HAMLET

A Study in Critical Method

HAMLET

A STUDY IN CRITICAL METHOD

by

A. J. A. WALDOCK, M.A.

Lecturer in English Literature in the
University of Sydney

CAMBRIDGE
AT THE UNIVERSITY PRESS
1931

CAMBRIDGE
UNIVERSITY PRESS

University Printing House, Cambridge CB2 8BS, United Kingdom

Cambridge University Press is part of the University of Cambridge.

It furthers the University's mission by disseminating knowledge in the pursuit of education, learning and research at the highest international levels of excellence.

www.cambridge.org
Information on this title: www.cambridge.org/9781107437692

© Cambridge University Press 1931

First published 1931
First paperback edition 2014

A catalogue record for this publication is available from the British Library

ISBN 978-1-107-43769-2 Paperback

CONTENTS

PREFACE

Many of Shakespeare's plays have puzzling features, but *Hamlet* is unique in that it provokes real uncertainty concerning the dramatist's main intention. Our efforts to discover what Shakespeare meant by it still go on. But if the accumulation of comment means anything, it means that we need no longer expect a solution in which all our perplexities will magically vanish. Some of the difficulties are in the play to stay.

My concern, in this attempt to estimate the present situation in *Hamlet* criticism, has been as much with procedures as with results. Nothing, plainly, can be more important in such a case than that we should be clear regarding the valid canons of critical method. That question is paramount.

Professor Sir Mungo MacCallum, though some of the points of view here taken are far from his own, will not refuse me the opportunity of paying homage to his Shakespeare teaching, which is of the kind that becomes part of one's life.

My sincere thanks are due to Mr R. G. Howarth, who kindly undertook to see this essay through the press.

A. J. A. W.

1931

CHAPTER I

THE RAISING OF THE PROBLEM

It would be extremely interesting to know exactly how an ordinarily well-educated and intelligent Elizabethan was impressed by the play of *Hamlet*. We can be fairly certain that he was impressed. We are left to infer that he was impressed in much the same way as the ordinarily well-educated and intelligent Englishman of to-day is impressed. But at least two allowances must be made. In the first place, he would have possessed, when he visited the theatre to see the play, an equipment which his fellow of to-day usually has not. In the second place, he would have visited the theatre unimpeded by an equipment which his fellow of to-day usually takes with him. He would have gone prepared to see a play with the structure, contents, or at least general drift of which he was already fairly familiar from a previous play (or previous plays) of the same name. For we cannot too frequently remind ourselves that *Hamlet* did not emerge from the void, that it was not a novelty: or if a novelty (for of course it was that) that it was a novel variation of a theme that had been tried before more than once, a theme that was apparently well known to the play-going public. Our *Hamlet* was possibly not even Shakespeare's first trial of the subject, but (it would seem) a second attempt at least. It seems likely that Shakespeare to some extent allowed for this foreknowledge of his theme on the part of his public; but this is a matter that we may take up again. At present, the point seems worth making that the story was familiar to an Elizabethan audience in a way in which to a modern audience it is not. *Hamlet*, to that audience, did not stand quite by itself; it had had forerunners; and no criticism is sound which does not take into account the possible consequences of this fact.

But we ourselves (or many of us) enjoy or suffer from another kind of foreknowledge, a foreknowledge in which the Elizabethan had no share. I mean, of course, the foreknowledge conferred by the criticisms and interpretations that now, for a century or so, have been gathering round the play. *Hamlet* is now thickly encrusted with them, so that it is a little difficult to get a direct sight of it. We have a number of *Hamlet* traditions. We have, without knowing it, been brought up Coleridgeans, or have unconsciously acquired a Goethean bent. The very word *Hamlet* now carries added connotations. The play has taken colour from every source, has been tinged by its passage through many minds. It is now very much more than itself.

All this may be, in a sense, to the good: or some of it. There are criticisms of *Hamlet*, no doubt, that we could spare: the play has inspired others that in themselves are a creation, that we would not, almost for their own sake, willingly let die. But it is all rather confusing. That is why it seems good that, periodically, we should attempt to take bearings. The discussion, after all, has progressed, if after the fashion of a spiral. Certain famous judgments of the play have been shown, almost to demonstration, and sometimes repeatedly, inadequate. It is well that this should be realised and that such judgments should be allowed to rest. The outlook has veered and shifted. It is useful to note in what directions. The following survey may perhaps serve to suggest, if only roughly and diagrammatically (and always from an unavoidably personal point of view) something of the present situation.

And, first, it is not without interest to glance at the raising of the problem. We do not know whether *Hamlet* perplexed the first audiences or not. We do know that we are unable to find any records of perplexity until more than a century after the performance of the play. We need not, perhaps, attach great significance to such a failure. But it is interesting to observe that the first commentators were not unduly worried by what puzzled them. Sir Thomas Hanmer, writing in 1736, noticed some difficulties. It is worth while noting what his difficulties were. They were the big problems, or what were to become the big problems. Usually it is an absence of apparent or sufficient motivation that he observes. Thus, why did Hamlet feign madness? Hanmer could not find that this was justified in Shakespeare's play and, in a very shrewd and noteworthy phrase, thought this "conforming to the groundwork of his plot" injudicious. Hanmer, again, was struck by what was to become the problem of problems. "There appears no reason at all in nature", he observed, "why this young Prince did not put the usurper to death as soon as possible", for the young man was represented as very brave and careless of his own life. "The case, indeed, is this," he goes on, "had Hamlet gone naturally to work, there would have been an end of the play. The poet, therefore, was obliged to delay his hero's revenge; but then he should have contrived some good reason for it." Such are the modest observations of one of our early critics of *Hamlet*. Naïve perhaps they are; but it is by no means certain, for all the wealth of later speculation, that we have got very far beyond them. The same quality of trenchant, if rather prosaic, commonsense, appears in the comments of Dr Johnson some thirty years later. It is interesting to note that he too was impressed by the imperfect motivation of the madness: "of the feigned madness of Hamlet there appears no adequate cause, for he does nothing which he might not have done with the reputation of sanity". This may not be strictly true. Later critics point out that the feigned madness at least was of service to Hamlet in that it allowed him when nearly beside himself to behave like a madman without causing surprise. This subtlety of understanding escaped Dr Johnson: and this fact again is worth noting. At all events it is remarkable that he and Hanmer both accept the difficulties very philosophically: they are there, and it is a pity, but no writer is perfect everywhere, and there seems not much more to be said. But how much more was to be said!

It was towards the end of the eighteenth century that the *Hamlet* problem, as a problem, began to emerge. In fact, by 1784, some ten years before Goethe wrote, and

some twenty years before Coleridge, it had been de-
fined clearly in its main aspects and some of the leading
theories had been suggested. Henry Mackenzie (1780)
was the first to lay notable stress, not only on what
seemed to him the doubts and hesitations, but also on
what he regarded as the "weaknesses" of Hamlet.
Much of Goethe's account is anticipated in Mackenzie's.
Hamlet is the "sweet Prince, the delicacy of whose
feelings a milder planet should have ruled, whose gentle
virtues should have bloomed through a life of felicity
and usefulness". Here is one main view of Hamlet's
character already sufficiently indicated. Even more interesting were some comments by Richardson, four
years later. Richardson makes one of the first attempts
to explore deeply into the roots of Hamlet's trouble and
could have given a lesson to many a later critic in
judicious emphasis. Whence does Hamlet's despon-
dency spring? Not from the death of his father, for,
says Richardson, "that was a natural evil and as such he
endures it". From political disappointments? Only neg-
ligibly, since "that he is excluded from succeeding immediately to the royalty seems to affect him slightly, for
to vehement and vain ambition he appears superior. He
is moved by finer principles, by an exquisite sense of
virtue, of moral beauty and turpitude". Then Richardson, taking the mere text as his guide, makes for the
core of the matter. "The impropriety of Gertrude's
behaviour, her ingratitude to the memory of her former
husband and the depravity she discovers in the choice of
a successor, afflict his soul and cast him into utter agony.

5

Here then is the principle and spring of all his actions."
Richardson deserves commendation for this. He anti-
cipates, as well, all the critics down to Bradley, in his
view of the feigned madness and its motive. Hamlet,
in Richardson's interpretation, is, to his own knowledge,
on the brink of madness. "Knowing that he must appear
incoherent and inconsistent, he is not unwilling to have
it believed that his reason is somewhat deranged, and
that the strangeness of his conduct admits of no other
explanation." Richardson, finally, is the discoverer of
excessive sensibility as the cause of Hamlet's indecision.
His account of the sparing by Hamlet of the King at
prayer might have set the traditional treatment. "The
sentiments that Hamlet expresses when he finds Claudius at prayer are not, I will venture to affirm, his real
ones. There is nothing in his whole character to justify
such savage enormity." How, then, is the episode to be
explained? Ingeniously, on the lines which were to become orthodox, Richardson reconstructs the event. Do
we not ourselves, he very plausibly asks, often allege
false motives for our behaviour? Do we not sometimes
do so almost without our knowledge? Apply all this to
Hamlet. Really, he is withheld "by the ascendant of a
gentle disposition, by the scruples, and perhaps weakness,
of extreme sensibility". But his sense of duty will not
allow him to acknowledge the truth even to himself.
"He alleges, as direct causes of his delay, motives that
could never influence his conduct and thus exhibits a
most exquisite picture of self-deceit." Richardson sums
up the whole tragedy: "[Hamlet's] original constitution

6

renders him unequal to the contest". How much later criticism is already implicit in such comments!

But we are now on the threshold of the Great Age and I will only pause for two brief remarks. It is, of course, strange that a play should ever have become a problem. Musical compositions, paintings, poems, even novels might well be or contain problems. But a play depends so much for its effect on ready comprehensibility. That a play which had been so successful should have had to wait so long until its true import began to be discovered, surely literary or dramatic history can contain few queerer phenomena than this. Of course, the strangeness has often been noted—then, generally, ignored or explained away. It seems to me difficult to explain it quite away. It is rather far-fetched, in this instance, to speak of artists who in the joy of creation work more subtly than they know, or of evasive meanings secreted within a disguise of melodrama. Nor is it a question of intricacies of detail, that might naturally require a more leisurely appreciation than the theatre affords. We cannot too often remind ourselves that the problem of *Hamlet* is the problem of the very central action of the piece. The difficulty, in ultimate terms, is to know what the play is really about. This is what is so very strange, that it should be difficult, or should have become difficult, to grasp the central drift of a play that has always been popular and successful.

In the second place, it is interesting to observe the methods of attacking this problem already adopted by Mackenzie and Richardson. Richardson, in particular, it will be noticed, yielded a very free rein to his imagination. In his discussion, for example, of the prayer-scene, where Hamlet spares Claudius, that was his deliberate method, to use his imagination to reconstruct a mysterious incident in the play. As we have seen, he reconstructs the incident very cleverly and no later commentator who has used the same method has been able to add much of importance to Richardson's interpretation of this scene. Only, let us note the word *reconstruct*, which his procedure inevitably suggests. We know that in the law courts crimes are frequently reconstructed; evidence is compiled, imaginations are used, judges and juries bring to bear their experience of human nature. Now, of course, in an appreciation of a play we cannot dispense with our imaginations, nor are we, ordinarily, required to lay aside our knowledge of human nature. But surely we should not in general be under the necessity of compiling evidence. Perhaps occasionally we might even have to do that. There are scenes in Shakespeare, we know, which are, by his own or another's fault, imperfect. There is nothing to be done with the last scene of *The Two Gentlemen of Verona*, if we do anything with it, but to try to reconstruct it. Parts of *Antony and Cleopatra* require some piecing together. But we are not, here, obviously dealing with such a scene. The prayer-scene in *Hamlet* is not garbled or incomplete; nor is it in Shakespeare's "shorthand" style. It bears every mark of being exactly what Shakespeare wished it to be: it is eminently finished and entire. Why, then, should we be obliged to reconstruct it? Why should any event,

8

in any well-written play, require to be reconstructed? It is already constructed. It carries (or should carry) its own meaning with it: for is not that precisely how drama differs from life? If dramas need to be put together as fragments of real life are put together in the law courts, why, it must occur to one, write dramas? Where is their advantage? It is fairly clear that this contradiction pervades a good deal of *Hamlet* commentary: it is produced by a radical fallacy in method.

CHAPTER II

GOETHE AND COLERIDGE

I have chosen Goethe and Coleridge as roughly typical of the next period of *Hamlet* criticism. Each began a certain tradition of thought and to one or other tradition most of what is said and written about the play even to this day belongs. Yet each view has been shown, with finality, unsatisfactory and incomplete.

Goethe is the most celebrated exponent of what has been called the sentimental theory of the hero of the play. This is the view that Mackenzie had already enunciated. Goethe expanded it and added a striking and very misleading image. Wilhelm Meister tells how he found the key to the Prince's character in the couplet:

> The time is out of joint: O cursed spite,
> That ever I was born to set it right!

He goes on: "In these words, I imagine, is the key to Hamlet's whole procedure, and to me it is clear that Shakespeare sought to depict a great deed laid upon a soul unequal to the performance of it. In this view I find the piece composed throughout. Here is an oak-tree planted in a costly vase, which should have received into its bosom only lovely flowers; the roots spread out, the vase is shivered to pieces.

"A beautiful, pure, and most moral nature, without the strength of nerve which makes the hero, sinks beneath a burden which it can neither bear nor throw off; every duty is holy to him—this too hard. The impossible is required of him,—not the impossible in itself, but the impossible to him. How he winds, turns, agonizes, advances, and recoils, ever reminded, ever reminding himself, and at last almost loses his purpose from his thoughts, without ever again recovering his peace of mind.

"Hamlet is endowed more properly with sentiment than with a character; it is events alone that push him on; and accordingly the piece has somewhat the amplification of a novel. But as it is Fate that draws the plan, as the piece proceeds from a deed of terror, and the hero is steadily driven on to a deed of terror, the work is tragic in its highest sense, and admits of no other than a tragic end."

This notable criticism (which was in essentials, nevertheless, not a marked advance on what had already been said by Mackenzie and Richardson) was a pattern and starting-point for a great volume of nineteenth-century comment. Gervinus, with modifications, adopted it: "an idealist, unequal to the real world". But the variations on the theme are numberless.

I suppose no portrait of Hamlet is quite so damaging to him as Goethe's. Both in the praise and the blame that it implies, it is shockingly unfair. The virtues it leaves him are precisely the virtues for which we have the coldest respect; the faults it alleges are the faults that (to our unregenerate nature) seem to have least perverse and saving grace. But if Goethe's impressions were so, what can we do? Is it not, in the last resort, by impressions that we must abide? But impressions can be tested. It is a matter of *text*, of attentiveness to what is actually said and done by Hamlet in the play. All feel the idealism of the Prince's nature; all realise his intense and exquisite appreciation of beauty and goodness; all comprehend the rarity of his soul. It is the suggestion of fragility that we do not like. We do not feel that to call his nature "beautiful" gives a perfectly just suggestion. The image of the "costly vase" strikes us as unfortunate. We resent his being denied "strength of nerve".

HAMLET.   Hold off your hands.
HORATIO.   Be ruled; you shall not go.
HAMLET. ...Still am I call'd: unhand me, gentlemen;
           By heaven, I'll make a ghost of him that lets me:
           I say, away! Go on; I'll follow thee.

An exchange such as this gives a vivid impression of the man and the impression is of a personality which can be very commanding and decisive. We may ignore for the time being those later and much stronger indications that his nature had streaks for which "beautiful" is an imperfectly descriptive term: his brutalities to Ophelia, his retaliation to Rosencrantz and Guildenstern. There are much milder passages in the play which are suggestive of reserve force, of an easy control and dignity. As Fortinbras felt, he has something "royal" about him. His ascendancy amongst his friends, we feel, proceeds from himself as much as from his rank: he would always effortlessly be chief. To put it shortly, he has, not only charm, but character—character, which Goethe would deny him, allowing him only "sentiment". No, there is no doubt that Goethe's pale and delicate Hamlet is none of Shakespeare's.

But something else about Goethe's criticism is noteworthy. Goethe set himself to imagine what Hamlet's nature was like before the play began and irrespective of the events of which it treats. In that occupation he neglected to note that by one of those events, before the Ghost appeared with his revelations, Hamlet's nature had been considerably affected. Surely, of all the strange phenomena of *Hamlet* criticism, none stranger can be found than the constant refusal, I will not say to attend to, but even to recognise the existence of, Hamlet's first soliloquy. For all that Goethe, and numberless critics between Richardson and Bradley, say of this soliloquy, it might not have been in their editions of the play. Yet one wonders whether any soliloquy could have quite the importance which, by all dramatic rights, belongs to this. It is in Scene II of the play that we have our first sight of Hamlet. During the earlier part of the scene he is silent, brooding as the others talk. His first utterance is a darkly ambiguous aside. There are a few more words from him, dejected or guarded, in any case significant of some deep trouble of mind. Then he is left alone and our expectancy is intense. Could any passage in the play be more significant than the soliloquy which we now overhear, this first confidential communication from Hamlet to ourselves? We naturally take it to be our key. From these first words we shall learn what the King and the Queen and the other people of the play do not know—what is the matter with Hamlet. This is what he says (I, ii, 129):[1]

> O, that this too too solid flesh would melt,
> Thaw and resolve itself into a dew!
> Or that the Everlasting had not fix'd
> His canon 'gainst self-slaughter! O God! God!
> How weary, stale, flat and unprofitable
> Seem to me all the uses of this world!
> Fie on't! ah fie! 'tis an unweeded garden,
> That grows to seed; things rank and gross in nature
> Possess it merely. That it should come to this!
> But two months dead! nay, not so much, not two:
> So excellent a king; that was, to this,
> Hyperion to a satyr: so loving to my mother,
> That he might not beteem the winds of heaven
> Visit her face too roughly. Heaven and earth!
> Must I remember? why, she would hang on him,
> As if increase of appetite had grown
> By what it fed on: and yet, within a month—
> Let me not think on't—Frailty, thy name is woman!—
> A little month, or ere those shoes were old
> With which she follow'd my poor father's body,
> Like Niobe, all tears:—why she, even she,—
> O God! a beast that wants discourse of reason
> Would have mourn'd longer,—married with my uncle,
> My father's brother, but no more like my father
> Than I to Hercules: within a month;
> Ere yet the salt of most unrighteous tears
> Had left the flushing in her galled eyes,
> She married. O, most wicked speed, to post
> With such dexterity to incestuous sheets!
> It is not, nor it cannot come to good:
> But break, my heart, for I must hold my tongue!

We need not stay at present to discuss the full meaning

[1] The references are to the "Temple Shakespeare" edition.

14

of this speech. Let us even grant that it is not quite all-illuminating, at least that it provokes us to wish to know more. Still, the force of it is unmistakable. Hamlet is in despair, is sickened even to a desire for death by something that has recently occurred. A terrific calamity has befallen him, his whole nature is upturned. And the particular origin of his trouble is made perfectly plain. It is the recent re-marriage (indecently hasty and incestuous re-marriage) of his mother. This event has changed the whole of life for him, the realisation of all that it seems to imply is poisoning his very soul. Well, whatever difficulties may remain, there seems here to be a datum of some importance. If it is given, at the outset of the play, that Hamlet has just suffered a really tremendous emotional shock, one of those shocks that impress the very personality, bruise and jangle the delicate machinery of the nerves, surely then if in some respects certain subsequent behaviour on his part, reactions of his to the demands of life, should appear slightly abnormal, we are in a measure prepared. It is made perfectly clear to us, in short, that the Hamlet who is called upon to avenge his father's murder is a Hamlet in an altogether exceptional condition of soul. Yet it might well be imagined, to read Goethe's analysis, that before the coming of the Ghost nothing whatever had occurred to trouble him, that his mood right up to that point had been crystal-clear. And from Coleridge's analysis one would gather no more.

Is Coleridge's Hamlet more faithful to the original

than Goethe's? Perhaps no theory of the Prince's character has had such a vogue as Coleridge's. It is still, without doubt, the most widely accepted. It is hardly too much to say that Coleridge's Hamlet has become part of general culture. Hamlet now almost connotes what Coleridge said about him. Many educated citizens have a very slight acquaintance with the play, but all educated citizens know that Hamlet meditated when he ought to have acted, that he was pre-eminently a philosopher, and that his resolution was sicklied o'er with the pale cast of thought.

It is not to be denied, of course, that Hamlet thinks a great deal; so (a fact which many commentators might appear to have overlooked) do most of Shakespeare's great figures. Lear, Othello, Macbeth are all philosophers. Coleridge, however, had in mind something rather broader than mere intellectualism. His notion was that in Hamlet we see an undue preponderance of all the faculties of reception, appreciation and understanding, and a corresponding deficiency in the powers of action: there was an "overbalance" both of the "contemplative" and of the "imaginative" sides of Hamlet's nature. Once again one is tempted to suggest that Hamlet has been rather unfairly singled out. We may grant that no character in the whole series of plays shows genius of thought or imagination comparable to his. We all feel (or should feel) with Mr Clutton-Brock[1] that in Hamlet there is some "extreme of experiencing power". His mind takes in more than the average man's, his range of

[1] *Shakespeare's Hamlet.*

16

feeling is much wider, he is one of those chosen of the earth who pre-eminently "understand". In all this he is a reflection of his creator, the fullest, no doubt, that we have. Nevertheless, other characters have their shares in such qualities, are, in their degrees, also reflections. Othello is a poet. When Taine, in the Coleridge tradition, affirms that Hamlet's is "a poet's soul, made not to act, but to dream", we wonder how it was that Othello's soul could "act". Is not Macbeth a dreamer? Yet deeds are not beyond him. The truth is that there is much false emphasis in the theory, as well as a core of misleading principle. As Professor Bradley pointed out, no firm reason exists why a man should not at once be thoughtful and practical. Many a deed of violence has been performed by persons of meditative propensities. But the most unsatisfactory quality of the theory is simply that it fails, once again, to accord with our full imaginative sense of Hamlet. Why should he be regarded, in his normal, essential nature, as "overbalanced"? The events of the play may overbalance him. We have seen, for example, what emphasis is laid, in the first soliloquy, upon the recent shock. But the Coleridgean view (like the Goethean) ignores all such intervening episodes, and posits an *inherent* incapacity, an original onesidedness.

What authentic signs are there of this? What, for example, is Hamlet's reputation in the play? Does anyone seem to regard him as an incapable bookworm? Ophelia's tribute may need qualifying, but it is there, it exists (III, i, 158):

O, what a noble mind is here o'erthrown!
The courtier's, soldier's, scholar's, eye, tongue, sword:
The expectancy and rose of the fair state,
The glass of fashion and the mould of form,
The observed of all observers, quite, quite down!

Mr Bradby[1] finds it difficult to believe that Hamlet's figure ever allowed him to be a glass of fashion, but, apart from this discrepancy, the text does not suggest that Ophelia's portrait is over-indulgent. He was a popular Prince: a favourite of the nation. He was keen in manly sports: how rivalry spurred him to meet Laertes with the foils (IV, vii, 103):

          KING.   Sir, this report of his
       Did Hamlet so envenom with his envy
       That he could nothing do but wish and beg
       Your sudden coming o'er, to play with him.

At the end,

       The soldiers' music and the rites of war
       Speak loudly for him.

But it is needless once again to conduct the refutation. There is no doubt that his nature was altogether more spacious, free and versatile than Coleridge's narrow definition allows.

And not only that. It was a good deal more formidable. We know how he treats Rosencrantz and Guildenstern. How can we miss the glee with which (III, iv, 205) he turns over his plans for that drastic (that *premeditated*) revenge:

                    Let it work;
       For 'tis the sport to have the enginer
       Hoist with his own petar: and't shall go hard

       [1] *Short Studies in Shakespeare.*

18

> But I will delve one yard below their mines,
> And blow them at the moon: O, 'tis most sweet
> When in one line two crafts directly meet.

One would say the satisfaction of a virtuoso in secret and dangerous enterprise. It is not as if all this were fatuity, as if he were some hysterical and misguided amateur. Nothing could be more professional than the efficiency with which he hoists them. Coolly (v, ii, 13) and with a genuine relish he recounts the details to Horatio: how, with his sea-gown scarf'd about him, he came upon deck in the dark and groped for his victims; how he withdrew the packet, took it down and unsealed it, discovering the nefarious project against his own life; how (not needing to think, the idea coming to him as by inspiration) he sat him down and devised a new commission, wherein the death of the bearers was presently ordered: how then, his luck standing by him, he resealed the package with his father's signet, which chanced to be a model of the other, and replaced it; and of the successful and terrible issue of the practice. "So Guildenstern and Rosencrantz go to't", Horatio comments pensively, and we remember Hamlet's cheerfully casual rejoinder:

> Why, man, they did make love to this employment;
> They are not near my conscience.

And how significant of his own respect for his practical powers is his conclusion:

> 'Tis dangerous when the baser nature comes
> Between the pass and fell incensed points
> Of mighty opposites.

"Mighty opposites"! Do we not agree, and feel ourselves that this Hamlet could indeed be, on occasion, a mighty opposite? But on no occasion, under no circumstances, would Coleridge or Schlegel grant him that possibility.

As for the other events of the English voyage, Hamlet had already related these in a terse letter to his friend (IV, vi, 12): "Ere we were two days old at sea, a pirate of very warlike appointment gave us chase. Finding ourselves too slow of sail, we put on a compelled valour, and in the grapple I boarded them: on the instant they got clear of our ship; so I alone became their prisoner".

Well, what is to be made of all this? This is the "academic dreamer" of Coleridgean critics; this is the youth who, in Professor Dowden's picture, "has slipped on into years of full manhood still a haunter of the University, a student of philosophies, an amateur in art, a ponderer on the things of life and death, who has never formed a resolution or executed a deed". It is to be hoped that we shall some day all perceive that this reconstruction of our Prince's character falls short of Shakespeare's meaning: shall agree with Bradley that the image "is inferior to Shakespeare's man and does him wrong".

Of course, as Bradley points out, the Coleridgean view has its descriptive truth. Hamlet as the play proceeds does appear to exhibit signs of morbid introspectiveness. We know how in the famous soliloquies he cross-examines himself. But that is hardly

Coleridge's point. Coleridge finds in such behaviour merely a heightening of a native tendency, merely the working out of an inborn disposition. Procrastination, according to Coleridge, was in the man's very blood. For the rest, the view has this additional interest, that it is an example of a kind of critical pitfall which even the greatest critics do not always escape, into which, perhaps, great creative critics are especially prone to slip: I mean the danger of imaginative substitution. Goethe's Hamlet reminds us of Werther. So, it has struck many people that the words in which Coleridge describes Hamlet might not inaptly have been used in description of himself: the portrait he sketches is ludicrously his own. In fact he says so.

CHAPTER III

BRADLEY

To pass by the criticism that appeared between Coleridge and Bradley may well seem inexcusable in however skipping a survey. But it is the safer course. If we were to plunge into that deep and dark abyss it is by no means certain that we should ever get out again. Not that brilliant things were not said in the nineteenth century. But on the whole, not much of note was added to what Goethe and Coleridge had already hinted. Our business, besides, is not so much with theories as with types of theories. Bradley is the next really attractive landmark.

But we may stop, perhaps, for a word at least on two theories that were elaborated within the interval. Bradley himself clears them from his path before coming to his constructive discussion. They are not important in themselves: they have a certain interest as object lessons.

The first attempts to show that Hamlet's obstacles were external: that he was hindered by the mere natural and inherent difficulties of the case. Now it is possible to make such a view sound very plausible: indeed, nothing easier. For consider the situation, how complex it is, how many things were to be provided for. Suppose the King killed out of hand, what next? What evidence has Hamlet that he acted justly? And how his difficulties have increased after the feigned madness! Now he has involved *himself* in a net, now he has something else to explain. For who will believe, supposing he kills the King, that the act was not committed in a fit of insanity? Will his explanation sound reasonable? In any case, what explanation precisely is he to give for the feigning of the madness? It has helped nothing. What deep device was it to further? Many things, too, will have to be cleared up in that speech of justification. What is to be said of his mother's part in the whole matter? It is impossible that her fame should remain untainted, yet to have it tainted is unthinkable. In short, the situation bristles with difficulties. Hamlet, to begin with, has a charge that will not be so easy to prove; he makes that prospective task heavier by himself acting queerly; he has a culprit whom he wishes to shield; and he is faced, besides all this, with the obvious practical problems that must accompany such a deed. Is it any wonder that he delayed? Of course, putting the case in such a way, it is no wonder. Unfortunately, it is not of the slightest consequence how very reasonably all such considerations are urged, *if the play does not urge them.* How much *Hamlet* criticism need not have been written if this self-evident principle had been kept in mind! How many plausible hypotheses crumble into dust at this easy test! We may argue with all the logic in the world that the matter must have been thus and thus, but if the play remains silent, we are where we were. Does the play remain silent about these practical difficulties which have been enumerated? Almost entirely. Then in the play they merely do not exist. There is really hardly the faintest suggestion that any of them were ever seriously in Hamlet's mind. We know that at the finish he is anxious that Horatio should tell his story for him so that he should not leave behind him a "wounded name". In another passage (II, ii, 588) he might seem, for a second, to be imagining himself pouring forth the story to the throng, "cleaving the general ear with horrid speech". It has been suggested (it is the veriest suggestion—we have simply no means of knowing) that when he speaks (IV, iv, 40) of

> some craven scruple
> Of thinking too precisely on the event

the "thinking" was of problems of ways and means. The evidence, in short, is negligible. On the other hand, we know well that he appears to assume, in speech after speech, the perfect practicability of the task: he has cause and strength and will and means to do't.

The question is only interesting for the lesson it enforces. It is very reasonable to suppose that Hamlet was confronted by grave external difficulties. It is not, perhaps, reasonable of the play to ignore them. But the play *does* ignore them, and we must rest content. The likelihoods of real life are not an infallible help in the appreciation of a play.

Let us pass to the second theory. The gist of this is that Hamlet was deterred by scruples of conscience. Now here again a plausible argument is very easily spun. We can sit back and imagine to ourselves: "Now if I were in that situation, called upon to perform such a deed, what should I feel?" By some such procedure as this, much even of present-day *Hamlet* criticism must surely be generated. Of course we arrive at solutions without difficulty. It is extremely natural to imagine a person (oneself) in Hamlet's case being troubled by conscience. If the simple theory seems uninteresting, we can without difficulty complicate it: posit an "unconscious conscience", a conscience that checks Hamlet without his knowing what is holding him back. Now, of all such theories the first and final demand is that they shall be immediately demonstrated by letter of text. I have known readers of the play, fresh with a theory, hurt when requested to do this: the theory was self-evident. But self-evidence is manifestly of no use here. The unconscious-conscience theory simply cannot be demonstrated: it is a theory, like so many others, "read into" the play. It is an interesting diagnosis; its only fault is that it is impossible to prove its application. It is needless to say that Hamlet himself gives no overt signs of being troubled by conscience: or if so, it is by a conscience working in the opposite direction. He *does* feel that he has been remiss in not killing Claudius, reproaches himself bitterly, meekly and guiltily accepts the Ghost's reproof. The one passage that it is possible to adduce seems to me to have not even the cogency that most opponents of the theory allow it. The passage is at v, ii, 63. Hamlet has been telling Horatio about the English voyage and of what he has discovered of the King's baseness. Horatio is deeply shocked: even he had not expected quite so much (v, ii, 63):

> Why, what a king is this!

And Hamlet, as one would turn to a friend after such a comment with a "Yes, will you tell me what you think of a rascal like that?", goes on:

> Does it not, think'st thee, stand me now upon—
> He that hath kill'd my king, and whored my mother;
> Popp'd in between the election and my hopes;
> Thrown out his angle for my proper life,
> And with such cozenage—is't not perfect conscience,
> To quit him with this arm? and is't not to be damn'd,
> To let this canker of our nature come
> In further evil?

Most critics appear to assume that Hamlet is really asking a question here of Horatio, and Bradley, with super-subtlety, finds in Horatio's rejoinder an implied reproof of the Prince's irrelevance. Hamlet, he thinks, is still searching unconsciously for excuses for delay and Horatio sees through him. But surely Horatio's

> It must be shortly known to him from England
> What is the issue of the business there

means merely that his thoughts have been running ahead on practical consequences; and Hamlet's own speech seems merely rhetorical and exclamatory. Horatio does not answer the question, simply because he knows that Hamlet is not seriously asking it. It is not that kind of a question. But the main point is perfectly clear. Hamlet throughout assumes not only that he *can*, but that he *ought* to kill the King, and these are assumptions of the play. It is owing chiefly to unguarded importations of modern feeling into our responses that such a theory as "conscience" could have arisen.

26

I pass now to a brief review of Bradley's own positive criticism. I suppose no one can fail to be impressed by the sanity, the care, the insight, the depth and reach of sympathy that are revealed in this celebrated discussion. By Bradley, Goethe and Coleridge both appear almost as dabblers. In Bradley's survey, science and imagination work in harmonious team. The result is thrilling.

Certainly few critics can ever have felt the play, and above all the personality of the hero, so keenly and completely. Little more perhaps remains to be said of the main impression which Hamlet, as a man, makes on us; the freedom and openness, the large-mindedness, the deep integrity; the idealism manifesting itself in a passionate appreciation of the beautiful, an equally passionate adoration of the good; the intellectual genius, appearing not in this or that specialised gift, but pervasively in all his responses and expressions. Bradley draws attention as well to what (in his view) might be elements of danger in this rich and varied nature: the tinge of "melancholic" temperament, in the old sense of the term: the liability (which might be conjectured) to deep changes of feeling and alternations of mood.

This, indeed, is Bradley's main concern: to explain, by a reconstruction of Hamlet's nature, how, in the circumstances, the delay came about. "In the circumstances" is now in the Bradleian critique, a vital phrase. It is not a question (as with Goethe and Coleridge) of merely defining a type of character, but of showing how, under that specific shock, the nature of which the first soliloquy discloses to us, a certain kind of temperament

27

might have suffered such damage that the task presently laid upon it would have been beyond its powers.

Nothing, again, could well surpass the fascinating ingenuity with which Bradley proceeds to show why the elements of this character did so react under those two dreadful trials. "If we still wonder, and ask why the effect of this shock should be so tremendous, let us observe that *now* the conditions have arisen under which Hamlet's highest endowments, his moral sensibility and his genius, become his enemies. A nature morally blunter would have felt even so dreadful a revelation less keenly. A slower and more limited and positive mind might not have extended so widely through its world the disgust and disbelief that have entered it. But Hamlet has the imagination which, for evil as well as good, feels and sees all things in one. Thought is the element of his life, and his thought is infected. He cannot prevent himself from probing and lacerating the wound in his soul. One idea, full of peril, holds him fast, and he cries out in agony at it, but is impotent to free himself ('Must I remember?' 'Let me not think on't'). And when, with the fading of his passion, the vividness of this idea abates, it does so only to leave behind a boundless weariness and a sick longing for death.

"And this is the time which his fate chooses. In this hour of uttermost weakness, this sinking of his whole being towards annihilation, there comes on him, bursting the bounds of the natural world with a shock of astonishment and terror, the revelation of his mother's adultery and his father's murder, and, with this, the demand on him, in the name of everything dearest and most sacred, to arise and act. And for a moment, though his brain reels and totters, his soul leaps up in passion to answer this demand. But it comes too late. It does but strike home the last rivet in the melancholy which holds him bound.

> The time is out of joint! O cursed spite
> That ever I was born to set it right,—

so he mutters within an hour of the moment when he vowed to give his life to the duty of revenge; and the rest of the story exhibits his vain efforts to fulfil this duty, his unconscious self-excuses and unavailing self-reproaches, and the tragic results of his delay."[1]

Bradley proceeds, then, to justify his diagnosis in detail. It is a very subtle and interesting diagnosis, and it must be admitted that it accords far more satisfactorily with our impressions than any of the theories we have yet considered.

And yet, is it quite satisfactory? I will not pause at present to elaborate an initial objection, but would nevertheless ask the reader to observe that the whole criticism finds its starting-point in a certain assumption. Bradley assumes, as self-evident, not only that Hamlet is irresolute, but that this irresolution is of the very essential stuff of the play: that the irresolution, in short, is what the play is essentially about. Now this, although it may seem rash at this time of day to make such a suggestion, is not quite a self-evident truth. Even if we grant (as of course we must) the existence of delay on Hamlet's part,

[1] *Shakespearean Tragedy*, p. 119.

it still remains true (as Bradley himself was at pains to point out) that most people who see the drama performed do not bother themselves greatly about this delay, and do not question themselves seriously as to its cause. It would appear then that the delay is not absolutely self-evident. It is not; and, really, any theory of the cause of delay in this play should logically be preceded by a demonstration that the delay exists: I mean that it exists as a prominent feature of the design of the piece, amounting to a problem. It is the weakness of the Bradley theory, as indeed of all similar theories, that it neglects first to establish the problem which it seeks to solve. I return to this matter.

But, even granting the problem as Bradley assumes it, is his explanation of the delay perfectly convincing? When all is said and done, why was it inevitable that Hamlet's reactions should be just so? He has, we know, after his dreadful disillusionment, a "sick longing for death" and a "boundless weariness". We can well believe that the second revelation "strikes home the last rivet" in his melancholy. But why should the issue be, so necessarily, a paralysis of the will? Even his burdened moan—

> The time is out of joint: O cursed spite,
> That ever I was born to set it right!—

does not imply, very clearly, a feeling that his task will be beyond him. He may not dance lightly to meet such a task. He may well feel bowed beneath a despair that was already heavy for bearing. His duty, we may understand, will be joyless, for joy has departed from this world become black. But the words do not definitely suggest that he fears inadequacy as such: he is "born to set it right": nothing hinders us from feeling that the task will somehow yet be performed.

Again, it is not altogether easy to understand why, in the Bradleian reconstruction of the case, inaction should be the sole probable response of Hamlet's nature to this demand. With this feeling of "no, no, no life", this deep disgust with all things human, this boundless despair, his impulse, one would think, might have been just as conceivably towards sweeping and all-ending violence. To make a finish with this business, and then with life itself; to execute this last duty, and then to find deliverance for ever, in self-slaughter, from the loathsomeness of existence: why should not this have been an equally likely effect? It is not as if an act of *resolution*, in the ordinary sense, was required: an act of *desperation* would have been sufficient. When, with his whole being "sinking towards annihilation" there came upon him this new horror and the demand linked with it, can one not imagine him, in the very excess of the added torture, impelled to "arise and act", dreadfully and once and for all? We know, of course, that he does, through the play, exhibit remarkable bursts of energy. Bradley allows for these, finding "those quick decided actions of his" to be "the outcome of a nature normally far from passive, now suddenly stimulated". Precisely, and in any such mood he might, most naturally, have killed the King. Indeed, in one such mood he does kill him—theoretically—when he plunges his blade through the curtained body of Polonius.

Bradley's explanation, in short, does not seem satisfactorily to establish "delay" as the obvious sequel of Hamlet's mental sufferings. Bradley is throughout concerned with showing why Hamlet's special temperament constituted a "danger" to himself, why his highest endowments might, under certain circumstances, become his "enemies". But it seems almost as plausible to imagine his temperament, under these same circumstances, as an asset. For such an act as Hamlet had to perform, "normality" was not altogether required. The strain under which he laboured, the sick despair infecting him, might themselves have simplified the task, itself not, in every sense, a normal one. I do not urge these considerations as dramatically very important, but rather as suggesting some failure on the part of Bradley's theory fully to account for the case even as he imagines it.

But perhaps more interesting than the theory itself is Bradley's justification of it by the plot. Here a certain fallacy in method seems to become apparent, and a principle is raised of the first importance.

The late Mr A. B. Walkley, in his review of *Shakespearean Tragedy* on its first appearance, noted a tendency in it to treat the *Hamlet* story as if it had actually occurred in real life, as if it were, authentically, *le cas Hamlet*. Now surely the principle here is very simple. We understand quite well that no creative artist can body forth convincing images of men and women without, in some degree of completeness, feeling those men and women as living. It is quite intelligible that what a dramatist or a novelist tells us about his characters may be only a selected fragment of his own total experience of them. We know, too, that our own imaginative response to play or novel is not complete until we have also, in our degree, felt such characters as alive. All this is easily granted. It does not alter the fact that a drama differs in certain essential respects from a slice of actuality and is not amenable to quite the same kind of handling.

One is reminded of the attitude of some readers to detective stories. How does one guess the criminal in a detective story? If the incidents and the people were in real life, one's suspicions, of course, could range over a very wide field. And some readers really seem to conduct their guess-work on this assumption and make the wildest conjectures. Their conjectures, if the story were real, would often be very reasonable. They are only wild because the events are not in the outer world, but in a book. In a book, there is a very much shorter cut to solutions and the problem itself is quite different. It is, plainly, to master the author's design. In the book, if one carefully notes the suggestions, the implied eliminations, it is of course seen by page so and so that a certain character *must* be the culprit; not always because of inherent likelihood but because of an artistic necessity. We make, naturally, one proviso. We must be given a chance. Our author must have the literary integrity to keep to his design. The design that at the last moment is deliberately falsified does not amuse us.

The point, however, is very clear. Drama is *not* history, and it is, above all, not raw material for history. Yet again and again it is noticeable that Bradley is assuming the historical occurrence of the events of the play. The events afford him openings for calculation: on the *basis* of the play he reconstructs what *really* happened.

The result is that he falls into various kinds of temptation. He is tempted, for example, to a super-subtlety that unearths impossible distinctions—impossible, at least, to the theatre. Thus, he qualifies Hamlet's joy in the success of his play. Hamlet exults in this success, "not really because it brings him nearer to his goal, but partly because it has demonstrated his own skill". We may thoroughly agree that Hamlet's triumph is, partly, that of the contriver who sees his contrivance most beautifully work. But to assert, from the impressions of this scene alone, that Hamlet is not really glad that he has proved the King's guilt, seems altogether too much. Bradley does not rely on the impressions of this scene alone. Even so, there is a limit to our powers, while a play is running, of putting two and two together—the two's being gathered from here, there and everywhere, some of them from scenes yet a long way ahead. The natural effect of the scene (reinforced by Hamlet's exclamations to Horatio after his test is over: "O good Horatio, I'll take the ghost's word for a thousand pound. Didst perceive?... Upon the talk of the poisoning?") is that of the Prince's exultant satisfaction at having confirmed the Ghost's charges.

Bradley, again, makes a use of his imagination, at times, that is scarcely legitimate. He uses it to supplement, as well as illumine, the play. He bridges gaps with it, fills in omissions. So, he shows how Coleridge's theory has its relevance: Hamlet, in his melancholy, weaving pretexts for inaction, going a weary round of self-dissection: "those endless questions (*as we may imagine them*) 'Was I deceived by the Ghost? How am I to do the deed? When? Where? What will be the consequence of attempting it—success,—my death, utter misunderstanding, mere mischief to the state? Can it be right to do it, or noble to kill a defenceless man? What is the good of doing it in such a world as this?'" But Bradley himself admits that in the text there is not so very much about that "excessive but useless mental activity" of which Coleridge speaks, and, as for these imaginary questions, we have very little means of knowing whether Hamlet asked them of himself or not. The fact that we are left to conjecture them shows that they cannot, in any case, be of great importance in the play. It is the same (an interesting matter, which I take up again) with the time-durations. Bradley points out that, judging from certain hints, a two months' interval is to be assumed between Acts I and II. We have, then, to infer Hamlet's behaviour during this pause. All he has done, apparently, is to put on a feigned madness. That is, he has been delaying all this time, plunged, no doubt, in "bestial oblivion", or trying to convince himself that he has doubts about the Ghost. But I think it is fairly clear that in reading, still more in seeing, the play, that

35　　　3-2

interval slips by almost without notice. The two months' break is missed (as I hope will be seen later) from another plane of the drama. As far as Hamlet is concerned, the interval is practically negligible: its dramatic existence is not marked. That means that it is worse than superfluous to set ourselves to imagining what Hamlet was doing within it.

But there are two passages of which the Bradleian account is especially interesting. I give them a chapter to themselves.

CHAPTER IV

THE PRAYER-SCENE AND THE
PLAY-SCENE

The first is the famous prayer-scene. Hamlet, it will
be remembered, has received ample confirmation from
the conduct of the King at his play that the Ghost spoke
truth. He receives word now that the Queen wishes to
see him. He stops for a moment, after the others go out,
to express the hot emotions consuming him (III, ii, 405):

'Tis now the very witching time of night,
When churchyards yawn, and hell itself breathes out
Contagion to this world: now could I drink hot blood,
And do such bitter business as the day
Would quake to look on. Soft! now to my mother.

Then he leaves for his mother's room, and on the way
comes across the kneeling Claudius. This is his speech
(III, iii, 73):

Now might I do it pat, now he is praying;
And now I'll do't: and so he goes to heaven:
And so am I revenged. That would be scann'd;
A villain kills my father; and for that,
I, his sole son, do this same villain send
To heaven.
O, this is hire and salary, not revenge.
He took my father grossly, full of bread,
With all his crimes broad blown, as flush as May;
And how his audit stands who knows save heaven?
But in our circumstance and course of thought,
'Tis heavy with him: and am I then revenged,

To take him in the purging of his soul,
When he is fit and season'd for his passage?
No.
Up, sword, and know thou a more horrid hent:
When he is drunk asleep, or in his rage,
Or in the incestuous pleasure of his bed;
At game, a-swearing, or about some act
That has no relish of salvation in't;
Then trip him, that his heels may kick at heaven
And that his soul may be as damn'd and black
As hell whereto it goes. My mother stays:
This physic but prolongs thy sickly days.

Now what is to be made of it? It is instructive to
remember how Richardson set about explaining the passage. He assumed, to begin with, that it stood in need of
interpretation. Hamlet's expressed sentiments are not
his real ones: "there is nothing in Hamlet's whole character that justifies such savage enormity". The speech,
in short, is too horrible ever to have been genuinely re-
presentative of Hamlet. It is some sort of a disguise
thrown up by his unconscious self. Just as the profligate
imposes on his own understanding in making his enor-
mities, even to his own eyes, pass for manliness of spirit;
just as the miser, "when he indulges his love of wealth,
says and believes, that he follows the maxims of laudable
economy", so Hamlet excuses to himself his natural
mercy by covering it in this hideous garb. Professor
Bradley, of course, does not follow Richardson in all
these details. When Richardson affirms that "there is
nothing in Hamlet's whole character that justifies such
savage enormity" he is simply not remembering the play
clearly. We think once more of the Hamlet who was to

take vengeance on his treacherous friends; the Hamlet who "lugs the guts" of the slain Polonius into the neighbour room. There *is* in the Hamlet we see a strain of savagery: the terms of the speech are not in themselves at all inconsistent with a side of his (present, jangled) nature that is exhibited more than once. And, again, as Bradley objects, nothing could be more unfaithful to the play than to minimize the intensity of Hamlet's hatred of the King. He has, as Bradley well puts it, almost a "phobia" of the subject: can hardly bear to think of the King for hatred: this "remorseless, treacherous, lecherous, kindless villain", this "bloody, bawdy villain", this soul "damn'd and black", this "slave", this "vice of kings", this "cut-purse of the empire and the rule", this "king of shreds and patches". No, there is assuredly no reason for believing that the horrible sentiments of this speech are not authentically and profoundly Hamlet's. Bradley, however, finds still a reason for rejecting the surface value of the words. The reason is, not that Hamlet's sentiments are horrible, "but that elsewhere, and also in the opening of his speech here, we can see that his reluctance to act is due to other causes". Take the opening of the speech again:

> Now might I do it pat, now he is praying;
> And now I'll do't: and so he goes to heaven:
> And so am I revenged. That would be scann'd.

"The first five words he utters 'Now might I do it' show that he has no effective desire to 'do it'." Thus Bradley. But surely this is the very ecstasy of sophistication. "Now *might* I do it": that little *might*! But whoever in an audience could have taken such a hint as that; whoever, reading the play with unbiased mind, could possibly check at such a subtlety! How strange that it should have been Professor Bradley who uttered this dictum: "Shakespeare wrote primarily for the theatre and not for students, and therefore great weight should be attached to the immediate impressions made by his works"! "Now might I do it pat": in other words, here is the very opportunity I have been looking for, here and now is my chance. "And now I'll do't": is there here some laborious "endeavour at a resolution", or is it in the most natural way in the world, the thought stiffening itself for the deed? It will be remembered that Hamlet is thinking quickly: he has come accidentally upon the King: he is to decide in a matter of seconds if he will choose this or another occasion (and there is no suggestion that occasions were scarce). Then, as he is on the brink of action, a counter-thought suddenly strikes him: "and so he goes to heaven": the irony of such a revenge! And in the rest of the speech this second thought slowly prevails. By line 87 he has reconsidered: he decides:

    No.
    Up, sword, and know thou a more horrid hent.

I feel that the sequence of the speech is in every detail simple and clear: it is a speech with a plain and obvious meaning; and it is something of a responsibility to refuse obvious meanings in a Shakespearean play.

This is really a test-passage of great importance, and I follow the matter a little farther. Bradley himself admits that the actability of the incident, in the sense in which he interprets it, is at least questionable: "in the little sentences that follow [the first five words], and the long pauses between them, the endeavour at a resolution, and the sickening return of melancholic paralysis, *however difficult a task they set to the actor...*": difficult task indeed, and one wonders when performed. But not so difficult, Bradley thinks, for the reader: such meanings are plain enough to him. But surely this is begging the question. The plain meaning is the meaning which the passage bears on its face. The Bradleian meaning, even if it were the true meaning, is certainly not the plain meaning. And it cannot be too emphatically urged that the onus is on the critic, in such a case, to demonstrate beyond doubt the subtler significance he finds. Is it really possible, in the present instance, to demonstrate such a significance? I find it interesting that a critic like Mr Clutton-Brock, of a decidedly Bradleian temper, should yet abandon any attempt to cover the nakedness of this passage with his theory.

Mr Clutton-Brock, however, while declining to discover tricks of the unconscious in Hamlet's behaviour, believes that we should see him at least trying to work up to a rage and failing. Here seems to return, in a slightly different form, that old conviction of Richardson that Hamlet simply could not be meaning what he was saying. The truth is that the incident, if it does not involve the unconscious in Hamlet, provokes certain responses from the unconscious in us. The chance offered to Hamlet is, as Bradley rightly observes, a repulsive chance—to us. We shrink from his accepting it. We could not help thinking less of him if he did accept it (although contradictorily, we are asked also to think less of him because he did not). The whole incident, to our present feelings, is strange, and Hamlet's scruples, as he expresses them, strike no very sympathetic chord. To put it in a word, the theology of the speech impresses us as incredibly primitive. That it is primitive is readily granted. But it can make no difference, Hamlet is by no means the only Elizabethan character who is made to utter sentiments of this kind.[1] Their primitiveness is merely to be accepted. We are all tempted to over-modernise Hamlet. Near as we feel him to be to ourselves, he still remains a literary creation of some years in the past. It is a passage like the present that should remind us, even if somewhat to our disturbance, of this truth.

As for the rage which, according to Mr Clutton-Brock, Hamlet here tries in vain to inflame in himself, his mood was evident enough when we last saw him. That was merely a few moments before, when he stopped to give vent to the passion of vengefulness within him:

> now could I drink hot blood,
> And do such bitter business as the day
> Would quake to look on.

---

[1] Professor J. Le Gay Brereton points out to me "how keen the gentlemanly ghost of Andrea was to have his enemies eternally punished 'Where none but furies, bugs and tortures dwell'".

Of course it is urged that such slaughterous breathings-out are meant to be in pointed contrast with his conduct when the opportunity occurs. But is such a meaning really conveyed? Is it not simpler to accept the words, once again, at their face value? The success of his play, the manifest guilt of the King, have left him burning with re-generated hate. He *is* ready for bitter business. The occasion offers, and he is about to accept it. Then the qualm comes, itself evidence of the intensity of his feeling, and he postpones this chance of a vengeance too mild: meaning every word he says. If such a literal acceptation, after the elaborate reconstructions which have become familiar to us, now seems almost crude, it cannot be helped.

It may be added that Bradley does not profess to derive the full import of this passage from itself alone: we refuse, he says, to accept Hamlet's own version of his motive in sparing Claudius, because "elsewhere, and also in the opening of his speech here, we can see that his reluctance to act is due to other causes". Now this leads us farther and I must reserve until a later chapter a discussion of such suggestions. My point here is that the reluctance, except by impossible sophistication, cannot be understood in the passage as it stands. And one is justified in feeling, besides, that only enormously powerful suggestions, elsewhere in the play, could bring to the surface, in this passage, the meaning that Bradley sees in it.

Let us pass to the second passage, also of great importance. It is the speech in which Hamlet announces

43

his plans for that play, the sequel of which we have been considering—ii, ii, 575:

Now I am alone.
O, what a rogue and peasant slave am I!
Is it not monstrous that this player here,
But in a fiction, in a dream of passion,
Could force his soul so to his own conceit
That from her working all his visage wann'd;
Tears in his eyes, distraction in's aspect,
A broken voice, and his whole function suiting
With forms to his conceit? and all for nothing!
For Hecuba!
What's Hecuba to him, or he to Hecuba,
That he should weep for her? What would he do,
Had he the motive and the cue for passion
That I have? He would drown the stage with tears
And cleave the general ear with horrid speech,
Make mad the guilty and appal the free,
Confound the ignorant, and amaze indeed
The very faculties of eyes and ears.
Yet I,
A dull and muddy-mettled rascal, peak,
Like John-a-dreams, unpregnant of my cause,
And can say nothing; no, not for a king,
Upon whose property and most dear life
A damn'd defeat was made. Am I a coward?
Who calls me villain? breaks my pate across?
Plucks off my beard, and blows it in my face?
Tweaks me by the nose? gives me the lie i' the throat,
As deep as to the lungs? who does me this?
Ha!
'Swounds, I should take it: for it cannot be
But I am pigeon-liver'd and lack gall
To make oppression bitter, or ere this
I should have fatted all the region kites
With this slave's offal: bloody, bawdy villain!

44

Remorseless, treacherous, lecherous, kindless villain!
O, vengeance!
Why, what an ass am I! This is most brave,
That I, the son of a dear father murder'd,
Prompted to my revenge by heaven and hell,
Must, like a whore, unpack my heart with words,
And fall a-cursing, like a very drab,
A scullion!
Fie upon't! Foh! About, my brain! Hum, I have heard
That guilty creatures, sitting at a play,
Have by the very cunning of the scene
Been struck so to the soul that presently
They have proclaim'd their malefactions;
For murder, though it have no tongue, will speak
With most miraculous organ. I'll have these players
Play something like the murder of my father
Before mine uncle: I'll observe his looks;
I'll tent him to the quick: if he but blench,
I know my course. The spirit that I have seen
May be the devil; and the devil hath power
To assume a pleasing shape; yea, and perhaps
Out of my weakness and my melancholy,
As he is very potent with such spirits,
Abuses me to damn me. I'll have grounds
More relative than this. The play's the thing
Wherein I'll catch the conscience of the king.

This is Bradley's comment: "Nothing, surely, can
be clearer than the meaning of this famous soliloquy.
The doubt which appears at its close, instead of being
the natural conclusion of the preceding thoughts, is
totally inconsistent with them. For Hamlet's self-reproaches, his curses on his enemy, and his perplexity
about his own inaction, one and all imply his faith in the
identity and truthfulness of the Ghost. Evidently this

sudden doubt, of which there has not been the slightest trace before, is no genuine doubt; it is an unconscious fiction, an excuse for his delay—and for its continuance".[1]

Now, in the first place, it is very important to recognise that Hamlet's doubt, whether it is genuine or not, is at least based on legitimate grounds. Here, again, our modern view requires some readjustment. There is no difficulty in obtaining information about the Elizabethan attitude to the supernatural.[2] All the suspicions that Hamlet expresses here had their root in popular belief. He is perfectly orthodox in his demonology. When Hamlet alleges, as his reason for obtaining confirmation, that the spirit that he has seen may be the devil, he is alleging something that, in itself, is extremely likely. It is also quite true, as he says, that the devil has power to assume a pleasing shape. It is, finally, only too probable that, supposing this Ghost were diabolic, he would have selected this time of lowered resistance in Hamlet, of weakness and melancholy, for attacking him. All these considerations, to us, seem far-fetched. We do not sympathise with such reasons, as we do not sympathise with the sentiments of the prayer-scene. It is easy for us to see in such arguments thin excuses. Would it have been as easy for an Elizabethan audience to see in them thin excuses: arguments so clear, so logical, so well-founded in doctrine and experience?

[1] *Shakespearean Tragedy*, p. 131.
[2] See Lavater, *Of Ghostes and Spirites walking by nyght*, edited by J. Dover Wilson and May Yardley, and the discussion in Lily B. Campbell, *Shakespeare's Tragic Heroes*.

Of course the doubts do come somewhat unexpectedly (though Horatio, by his own previous fears, has in a sense prepared us for them[1]). The transition is abrupt. As Professor Bradley says, those curses, those reproaches, those perplexities that make up the bulk of the soliloquy, one and all imply complete confidence in the genuineness and veracity of the apparition. Nor have we had any previous warnings (at least on Hamlet's part) of these doubts: they appear suddenly out of a clear sky. All this is true enough. Yet it is impossible to believe that if Shakespeare had really desired to convey such a meaning as Bradley finds he would not have made it more unmistakable. As it stands, it is extremely mistakable. The explanation, surely, is much simpler; and it is an explanation that covers, quite adequately, certain other passages from which intricate deductions have been drawn. It is merely that the workmanship is rather transparent. Is it not fairly clear? The next major event due in the plot is the play-scene. The concluding parts of this soliloquy provide the bridge to that scene. It is not, perhaps, a thoroughly sound bridge; if we step heavily on it, it gives alarmingly. If we slip by more lightly, it serves well enough. In line 617 we have the preparatory announcement:

> Hum, I have heard
> That guilty creatures, sitting at a play....

We may call this, if we will, Shakespeare's pretext for the play-scene. It is rather an abrupt way of bringing

[1] "What if it tempt you toward the flood, my lord?..."
(I, iv, 69).

47

the play-scene in. But what audience in the world would pounce on it as Hamlet's pretext for inaction? On the contrary, it promises present action, and our anticipations leave us no time for wondering further. In any case we hear the words:

> I'll observe his looks;
> I'll tent him to the quick: if he but blench,
> I know my course.

What more, at this moment of the play, have we a right to expect? Then follow the plausible reasons for doubt.

There is one other thing. We suspect Hamlet's motives. Why is not Horatio made to suspect them? He agrees quite simply to the plan (III, ii, 93). Then, after the play is over, and as the company breaks up in confusion, Hamlet turns excitedly to his friend (III, ii, 297):

HAMLET. O good Horatio, I'll take the ghost's word for a thousand pound. Didst perceive?
HORATIO. Very well, my lord.
HAMLET. Upon the talk of the poisoning?
HORATIO. I did very well note him.

I will not stop to discuss the suggestion that Horatio is here speaking "dryly"!

It seems clear, in short, that the Bradleian interpretation of this speech rests on a balancing of afterthoughts. It is not the meaning which the passage naturally and immediately carries. When we scrutinise this passage closely, we are struck by the inconsistency between beginning and end. If we have already in our mind ideas about the cause of Hamlet's irresolution, we can find in this inconsistency ingenious support for them. But I doubt if any reader, perusing the passage for the first time, in its natural order, and without prejudice, is really checked by the inconsistency: and still more that he would immediately infer from it that Hamlet was inventing unconscious fictions. As for the playgoer, and above all for the Elizabethan playgoer, it is absurd, surely, to imagine that he could ever catch such a drift.

I have dwelt on these two well-known passages, partly because of their intrinsic importance, and partly because Bradley's fashion of dealing with them raises such interesting issues. To read Bradley apart from the play (or, for that matter, with the play) is to be entranced by an exposition built up with deft skill and masterly thoroughness. His *Hamlet* stands four-square: every join is neat, every buttress seems solid. It is only when one inspects a little more closely that one sees that some important members of this construction (a fascinating work of art) have suffered slight alterations from the Shakespearean design. They have, in a sense, actually been improved upon. Bradley's *Hamlet* is better than Shakespeare's: it is better in the sense that it has a firmer consistency, that it hangs together with a more irresistible logic. We have not yet fully surveyed the Shakespearean *Hamlet*, but even the passages just discussed might suggest that its build is more magnificently rugged: that the dovetailing is not always such a perfection, that not every pillar is so splendidly in line.

CHAPTER V

MOTHER AND SON

It was inevitable that Hamlet, sooner or later, should be psycho-analysed, for he is a perfect subject. It is, indeed, very interesting to note what the new psychology has to say about him.

We owe the major elucidation of him from this point of view to Dr Ernest Jones.[1] Jones first of all posits the impression which Hamlet makes as that of "a strong man tortured by some mysterious inhibition". Our business, then, is to discover the nature of this inhibition. Bradley's account is judged inadequate, for it is based on rather conventional ideas of the causes of deep emotion: it is not, according to Dr Jones, psychologically up-to-date: nor does it quite recognise that certain disproportion between cause and effect which appears in Hamlet's responses to his mother's re-marriage. Hamlet's sufferings (Jones rightly points out) have struck many people as being, even when all allowances are made for the idealism of his character, a good deal in excess of the occasion. We may grant that the marriage was offensive then as it would not be now: it was not only indecently hasty; it was incestuous. The point still remains that Hamlet is shocked in a way and to a degree that we can hardly help thinking abnormal. The question is, what does really produce this abnormal effect?

Jones then plunges in. With care and industry, and

[1] *Essays in Applied Psycho-Analysis.*

much shrewdness of observation, he collects the relevant data, assumes for his purpose that they have precisely the validity that would attach to a case in real life, and works out his solution. There are admittedly some difficulties, but they are for the most part only such as would occur to laymen. Thus, we must begin, of course, by assuming that Hamlet did not understand the nature of his inhibition: if he had understood it, it would not have been one. The ordinary person, accordingly, might feel some qualms about the practicability of penetrating to it. Jones, however, denounces this at once as a "pessimistic thought" and smiles at the simplicity of such a doubter. "Fortunately for our investigation, psychoanalytic studies have demonstrated beyond doubt that mental trends hidden from the subject himself may come to external expression in ways that reveal their nature to the trained observer." Nor is that all. It is equally possible that Shakespeare himself did not understand the nature of the inhibition that was stopping Hamlet. We reach in the end the startling, but to Jones only "apparent" paradox, that "the hero, the poet, and the audience are all profoundly moved by feelings due to a conflict of the source of which they are unaware".

But the audience, at least, if it will follow Jones, is not condemned to remain in unawareness and may presently understand the case far better than the dramatist. Let us consider it again. Hamlet does not know why he cannot act. He *can* act, in other matters, but not in this. His trouble is *specific aboulia*, his will power is restricted in one direction. He tries to explain his inability to himself, but his explanations differ and are therefore and for other reasons untenable. The real explanation is this. The mother's second marriage awakes into activity a slumbering memory. Hamlet, as a child, had had a passion for his mother. He had resented sharing this passion with his father. He had regarded this father as a rival and had secretly wished him out of the way, so that he might enjoy the monopoly of his mother's affection. The point is that such thoughts had been repressed. Now, in the murder of the father, these old repressed desires find their realisation; the stifled memories are rekindled; and the result is this terrible disturbance of soul, the cause of which Hamlet is far from knowing, but which we see as the "obscure aftermath of his childhood's conflict". And why cannot he kill his uncle? Because his uncle, the slayer of his father, is the symbol of his own repressed desires become victorious. His uncle is his buried self: to kill his uncle is to kill himself. He is only released from the mysterious band, set free to fulfil his duty, when himself brought to the door of death.

Here is realism in interpretation with a vengeance. But Jones does not let the matter rest quite there. He eludes our obvious comments by suddenly shifting his explanation a stage farther back. All this conflict in Hamlet is neither more nor less than the echo of a similar one in Shakespeare himself. Ultimately, it was Shakespeare who had the Oedipus complex, who hated his father as a rival, and would, in similar circumstances, have found it impossible to kill his uncle.

Two comments still seem relevant. In the first place one wonders where this principle, of an author's unconsciousness of his own purposes, might eventually lead us. Indeed, it has led us far in the present case. Jones makes light of such a perplexity, or rather, proclaims his creed with bravado. It is, he asserts, actually beside the point to enquire into Shakespeare's conscious intentions. So it is, he thinks, with the work of most great creative artists. The play is simply the form in which Shakespeare's deepest, unconscious feelings find their spontaneous expression. Now that there is some truth in such a view we may readily grant. We can easily think of writers to whom such phrases might seem to apply with greater aptness. But it is surely not going too far to feel with Jones that much of the stuff of *Hamlet* came from inspirations that took their origin in the "deepest and darkest regions" of Shakespeare's mind. No one would suggest at least that a writer needs to be able to supply a coherent psychological analysis, with terms complete, of the characters he creates: his business is rather to feel his characters very intensely. We can have no doubt, for all the perplexities of the play, that if ever Shakespeare did feel a character intensely, it was Hamlet. Nor does there seem a reason to refuse the suggestion, which Jones (after Bradley) makes, that the behaviour of Hamlet might well represent Shakespeare's sense of what his own behaviour in such circumstances could have been. There is no harm in having the notion, if we like it, that Shakespeare, while he would have extricated himself from Othello's difficulties with the greatest ease, could not have coped with Hamlet's problem. All this we may let pass. It is still a good deal to ask us to believe that not this or that touch, not an intimation here, a suggestion there, but the central plot of this play, depends on, *is*, a complex of the author's, the nature of which, the existence of which, were of course quite hidden from his conscious mind. One wonders what Shakespeare himself thought of Hamlet's symptoms; and seeing that, when he had produced them, he could gain no glimmer of an idea of what they meant (as of course by hypothesis he could not), why he did not become anxious about them. Even Jones will admit that, in all probability, Shakespeare was "not only inspired from the personal and intimate sources we have indicated, but was also influenced by his actual conscious experiences". It is conceded that there is something "conscious" in the play. And although, according to Jones, Shakespeare's Oedipus complex is rampant in other works, still it must surely be allowed that in many of his plays he seems to be writing in some considerable state of awareness. Why, in *Hamlet*, he should have departed from what seems to have been his usual practice (namely, of working as a more or less conscious artist) and have suddenly decided to abandon himself to the whims of his subconscious nature, is hard to see.

But even supposing it were so; even supposing that Shakespeare did try here to portray something which he could not himself understand; that the play, as Mr T. S. Eliot puts it, is "full of some stuff that the writer could

not drag to light, contemplate, or manipulate into art";
plainly in such a case our own understandings cannot be
of much use. The point, as Mr Eliot says, is that the
stuff is not dragged to light, is *not* manipulated into art.
If Hamlet has a complex, what business is it of ours?
When a complex is made into dramatic material it becomes our business, not before. And even to speak of
Hamlet's complex is to speak of something in another
dimension: it is a thing that has no being in the world of
our play. With as much reason might we set about explaining Macbeth's crime by an investigation of the
medical history of his grandfather. The reply, in short,
to all such attempts is that, whatever illumination they
may shed by the way, they are in bulk devoid of all
dramatic relevance.

Dr Jones *does* shed illumination by the way. It seems
to me that few investigators have laid emphasis so valu-
ably on an aspect of the play strangely ignored or under-
estimated in *Hamlet* criticism: I mean, using the term
in a rather special sense, its sexual quality. Goethe and
Coleridge, as we have seen, do not recognise the existence of such a quality in the play, and Bradley scarcely
seems to grant it the importance it deserves. Let us
return to that first soliloquy. Really, "moral shock"
hardly seems adequate to the impression this soliloquy
conveys. There is in some of the lines almost a physical
nausea. Hamlet is sick with disgust. He could retch
with the thought of the things his mother has been
doing. Now this impression seems of very great importance indeed. There is, if we like, something abnormal

in the quality of Hamlet's feeling. But, above all, it is no *abstract* feeling (although, as we know, the despair does universalise itself). The feeling is in its essential nature exceedingly intimate. And it does, surely, put us in mind strongly of the things on which Jones fixes his attention. There is a suggestion that Hamlet has received damage of a kind analogous to the damage sometimes revealed by the procedures of psycho-analysis. I see no possibility, in a dramatic appreciation of the play, of going much farther than this. That Hamlet seems to have been hurt in that most intimate relationship, the relationship between mother and son; that his trouble derives, in a narrower sense than is usually understood, from this source: we may surely go so far.

We may go farther. What is the play of *Hamlet* really about? It is, of course, about many things; we understand how various are its appeals. But what is it most deeply about? Irresolution? Surely there is something in the play deeper than that. If we answer the question by asking ourselves another one, What is it that Hamlet himself is most deeply concerned about?—What is it that above all other things dominates his soul?—we can have no doubt what we must say. It would be too much to affirm that, compared with his horror at his mother, the shock of the murder is a trifle: yet it is nearly true. If the centre of the equilibrium of the play is the centre of the equilibrium of Hamlet's soul, then it is clear where it must lie. He forgets his vengeance; but he remembers this other thing. How he remembers it! It is strange that so vital a strain in the play should not have received more attention: it is impossible not to feel it. The first soliloquy brings it home to us; it is from then onwards the underlying theme. With Hamlet the feeling is an obsession and we are never left for long without an indication of its presence. We hear from Ophelia presently (II, i, 88) how he came to her, grasped her wrist, and, with his hand o'er his brow, fell to such perusal of her face as he would draw it; then, after the soul-searching scrutiny, raised a sigh that seemed

> to shatter all his bulk
> And end his being.

It is as if already all womanhood has become suspect of the corruption he has discovered in his mother. A little later is the bitter gibing of the speech with Polonius (II, ii, 182): "Have you a daughter?....Let her not walk i' the sun: conception is a blessing; but as your daughter may conceive...". It is the same when next he meets Ophelia: the cruel harping on "honesty" (III, i, 103), the savage cynicism of "for wise men know well enough what monsters you make of them" (III, i, 143), the anguish that suddenly starts into his voice and makes us glimpse the abyss in his soul: "Go to, I'll no more on't; it hath made me mad" (III, i, 153). Here too is that same spreading and deepening of the disgust to include all life: "What should such fellows as I do crawling between heaven and earth?" (III, i, 129). We see him again soon in the play-scene. He and Horatio are supposed to be watching every movement of the King's features. How does he occupy himself? We remember how he lies down at Ophelia's feet and with what manner of jesting he passes the time. And then, the troubled Ophelia calling him "merry", instantaneously, and, as it were, automatically, comes the sarcastic rejoinder: "What should a man do but be merry? for, look you, how cheerfully my mother looks, and my father died within's two hours". Presently, "'Tis brief, my lord", comments Ophelia, of the play; the response is inevitable: "as woman's love". It is as if his experience has become woven into the very texture of his mind; he thinks of nothing else. The very word "mother" has become an instrument of torture to him and he invents ways of using it on himself: puns, innuendoes, cryptic jests (III, ii, 343):

ROSENCRANTZ. She desires to speak with you in her closet, ere you go to bed.
HAMLET. We shall obey, were she ten times our mother.

His good-bye to the King is a grotesque conundrum (IV, iii, 51):

Farewell, dear mother.
KING. Thy loving father, Hamlet.
HAMLET. My mother: father and mother is man and wife; man and wife is one flesh, and so, my mother.

The climax is reached in the scene in Gertrude's room, where his tormented spirit relieves itself in those bitter upbraidings. But what is most interesting to note is the quality of the dark thoughts and images that now gush forth. The loathsome broodings that had made his mind a hell now appear in all their hideousness in the light of day. It is a terrible and wonderful scene and in figure after figure ("batten", "compulsive ardour", frost that

58

burns, "rank sweat", "stew'd in corruption", "sty", "compost") we are made to see with what thoughts, what pictures, Hamlet had been living. We need not wonder much further about what came to him in the bad dreams. Perhaps most terrible, most touching of all, is that strangely intimate, urgent, pleading with the mother, that she should not return to the marriage-bed. He can scarcely relinquish this subject; it is as if it had fastened on his very soul.

It seems certain, too, that we must understand the mystery of his relations with Ophelia (so far as we can understand it) in the light of all this trouble. It is indeed rather a question of guessing than of understanding. The whole matter is left, perhaps with some deliberation, enigmatic. We seem justified in assuming that Hamlet loved Ophelia once, though even there we are given little chance of doing more than speculate on the quality and intensity of his love. It seems clear that the love, as we see it in the play, has been poisoned by some strange resentment, suspicion or hatred. The rest is left undetermined. But we do seem warranted, at least, in connecting this change with that other experience. All women fall under the ban. Perhaps we may go even farther. Those jeering allusions of Hamlet's to "conception"; those pitiful songs of Ophelia in madness; do such hints amount to anything? Is it suggested that Hamlet savagely tried Ophelia, to see if she was of the selfsame metal as his mother? It would at least have been natural, in this wreckage of his world, to turn and experiment bitterly on this last piece of seeming innocence, testing if it also were wreckable. If it were so, we can imagine what her death meant to him and gain, as Professor Allardyce Nicoll suggests, a new comprehension of the "It is no matter" mood of Act v. But we cannot pursue this. We are left with the conclusion that Shakespeare did not trouble or did not wish to make the Hamlet-Ophelia story plainer, and in face of his refusal are helpless.

CHAPTER VI

THE BACKGROUND OF THE PLAY

This helplessness that so often overcomes us in considering *Hamlet*—helplessness to know what we should think when the dramatist himself has not helped us to know—is itself interesting and important and suggests other lines of attack. Even before Dr Jones, declining to admit any such helplessness, had psycho-analysed Hamlet, some of these had been tried. Professor C. M. Lewis in his *The Genesis of Hamlet* had studied the play from what was then (1907) a new point of view. Starting from the well-established and conspicuous fact that *Hamlet* is a new play formed out of an old one (the old one itself deriving from variations of a still older story) he set himself to discover what might be discoverable concerning Shakespeare's original contributions to his plot. It seemed obvious that if Shakespeare, working on his given material, had changed this and added that, such changes and additions would be informative of his purpose. It was likely, too, that the very fact that he was working on given material would be found to have implications. In the re-fashioning, it was not beyond possibility that some of the old stuff should have failed of complete assimilation to the new: that here and there bad joins should have been made, threads have become a little tangled, the patterns at this point or that have been thrown into slight distortions. More recently, writers like Mr J. M. Robertson and Professor E. E. Stoll have conducted similar enquiries. Professor Stoll and Professor Schücking, besides, have emphasised the need of an historical attitude. Dramatic technique changes, presuppositions alter, and we may well go astray if we do not allow, in *Hamlet*, for an art-form that is, in some details, more primitive than ours; that is, at least different.

These methods of approach are of great interest and their results call for some discussion.

Let us first examine the relation of our play to its predecessors and their sources. It will not be necessary to describe these sources fully. The old story, appearing originally in the *Historia Danica* of Saxo Grammaticus, could have been read by Shakespeare in Belleforest's *Histoires Tragiques*. As for the various dramas, we know from Nashe's reference that there was a play on Hamlet as early as 1589. This old play, if we possessed it, might be of considerable assistance to us in our trouble. It is possible that the author of it was Thomas Kyd, whose *Spanish Tragedy* may at least suggest the kind of thing it was. Shakespeare seems to have revised this play, and we may see something of his earlier attempts at revision in the First Quarto *Hamlet*. If we do, however, we see them mangled by bad reporting, for the text of the First Quarto (or most of it) appears to have been taken down in shorthand from an actual performance of the play. Any inferences, therefore, from the First Quarto have to be made with this caution in mind. Besides the First Quarto we have two other texts of *Hamlet*: they are *our* texts: the Second Quarto and the Folio. The Folio version is the shorter and represents the play as slightly adapted for acting. It is usual to dismiss the differences between the Folio and Second Quarto versions as negligible. There is, however, one difference at least that seems to me significant. I shall note it later. Then one other document exists of relevance to our study. This is a German play on Hamlet, bearing the date 1710, but probably belonging to a much earlier period. It is called *Der Bestrafte Brudermord*. Its interest is that it may well preserve elements of that old lost English play of *Hamlet*.

Now here, in this collection, we might well expect to find some help. We do find it, but it is disappointingly meagre.

Take, first of all, the First Quarto. How much, from a comparison of this text with our standard text, is it possible to learn? Really, on our own central problem, almost nothing. We are helped, possibly, to clear up a few difficulties of minor importance. Thus, the question has often been raised whether the Queen was privy to the murder of her husband. With all her failings, she does not impress us with that kind of badness. But Hamlet, so it is sometimes said, understands it that way. In III, iv he makes the pass through the arras. The Queen exclaims:

> O, what a rash and bloody deed is this!

To which he replies:

> A bloody deed! Almost as bad, good mother,
> As kill a king, and marry with his brother.
> QUEEN. As kill a king!

Mr G. F. Bradby says: "She neither admits the charge nor denies it". Of course, by her words she does not, though we may well understand that her voice is full of shocked astonishment. But the First Quarto is quite explicit: "How! kill a King!" and then:

> I swear by heaven
> I never knew of this most horrid murder.

Now it is true that the Queen's part is in other respects slightly modified in the Second Quarto. But there is simply no indication that Shakespeare had this particular change in mind. As other things appear equal, we seem justified in assuming that the explicit intentions of the earlier version correspond with the rather less direct suggestions of the later. (Hamlet's behaviour, of course, gives no hint elsewhere that he cherished such a belief seriously, nor does he here proceed with the accusation.)

I think we may apply the same line of reasoning to that passage, previously discussed, where Hamlet comes upon the praying King and stays his hand. We have seen how Professor Bradley finds evidence, in the first few lines of the speech, of subconscious hesitancy. Hamlet has "no effective desire" to perform the deed, and his very words show it: "Now *might* I do it". Now this speech, in the First Quarto, is, in all essentials, the same. It is the same speech, as it might have been, under some difficulties, heard and reported. In it the important word "might" has disappeared. It goes:

> I so, come forth and worke thy last,
> And thus he dies; and so am I revenged:
> No, not so: he took my father.

It gives perhaps more plainly still the impression that the speech of the Second Quarto gives plainly: the dark joy at the opportunity; the imminence of the deed, the sword drawn from its scabbard; the sudden check, the dissatisfaction, the sword thrust back.

But when we come to questions of wider scope, we are not given much assistance by the First Quarto. This is true, above all, of the problem of problems. Hamlet himself makes much the same impression in the First Quarto as in the Second. There are certain differences of text, but it is not easy to draw inferences from them. Thus, the "To be" soliloquy is shifted a little in the Second Quarto. There may be (as Professor Stoll suggests) some advantage of suspense and climax in this displacement; there seems no very strong significance for character. It is rather more important to observe that in the First Quarto the "How all occasions" soliloquy (IV, iv, 32) is missing altogether. It is missing also, perhaps a still more interesting fact, from the Folio version. I return to this. Otherwise, the modifications hardly affect the chief issues. The First Quarto furnishes us with no important clues to Shakespeare's deeper designs.

What of the sources and of what can be gathered concerning the older *Hamlet*? It is clear at least that the story as it came to Shakespeare's hands was a story of comparatively crude build—of rather obvious motives and direct aims. In its oldest forms the narrative is one of revenge pure and simple. The murder is open and notorious; the madness of the avenger is assumed for cover; the avenger delays because he cannot help himself: there are serious difficulties—guards, courtiers about the King. In short, all is external and clear as day. It may be that in the lost play of *Hamlet* the clarity was already beginning to be obscured; but we may conjecture that the old lines were still followed and that the play was still one of downright and easily comprehensible revenge. Now, in Shakespeare, what has happened? We have, to begin with, the importation of almost a new central motive, for how we can deny centrality to the mother-son motive it is difficult to see. And what happens to *revenge*? Whether the task of welding the new motive to the old proved surprisingly irksome, whether it was that in the interest of his new ideas Shakespeare became absent-minded about the old groundwork, it is clear that the revenge theme in the final play has been considerably damaged: and this remains true apart from any theories we may cherish concerning the cause of the inaction. There are misfits. The old material seems here and there to bulge out awkwardly into the new play. Old consequences are retained, and sometimes do not have their proper causes. Episodes lose their *raison d'être* and inhere in the play like survivals.

We may note one or two of the most conspicuous examples. The madness is one. As we have seen, the madness in the original plot had point and logic. It was a shelter behind which the avenger would await his opportunity. Perhaps in the "Ur-Hamlet" the madness had already lost some of its logic. If the murder by now had been made secret, such a device would at least not have been so obviously useful. In the Shakespearean play it has become really puzzling. For how much, after all, can we say about it? We know the famous explanation. It is an emotional safety-valve for Hamlet: he had some subtle feeling that he would need it. The explanation is exceedingly attractive and we wish we could be sure that Shakespeare so meant it. But we cannot, after all, be quite sure. Certainly the scene of the "wild and whirling words" is wonderfully conceived. It is a scene that, apart from minor difficulties, is immediately convincing: the half-hysterical outburst after the Ghost's revelation, the drop from the tension to a buffoonery that strikes his companions as equally hysterical, his *silliness* as they question him—

> HORATIO. What news, my lord?
> HAMLET. O, wonderful!—

then the grotesque interlude with the subterranean Ghost, and, at the end, the returning melancholy. But it is doubtful whether the vivid impressions of this scene quite suffice to answer the question, why he put on the madness. There is that mysterious business of the swearing to secrecy; and then the instruction (I, v, 168):

> But come;
> Here, as before, never, so help you mercy,
> How strange or odd soe'er I bear myself,
> As I perchance hereafter shall think meet
> To put an antic disposition on,
> That you, at such times seeing me, never shall,
> With arms encumber'd thus, or this head-shake....

But why? we ask ourselves again. I think the conclusion is inescapable, that here is at all events a partial failure to assimilate, re-explain, original material. Nor can we help feeling that, compared with Shakespeare's own audiences, we are rather at a disadvantage. This swearing to secrecy, this assumption of the antic disposition, were familiar, time-honoured incidents. And though, in Shakespeare's new play, their old significances had almost disappeared, to the audiences, no doubt, they carried their old sanctions with them. They had become, as it were, institutional and could stand by their own prestige. It could not be detected, besides, until later in the play, that they had now become meaningless; at the moment they would seem natural enough. I feel that no other view is nearly so satisfactory. We *can* re-explain the antic disposition; but we do it without full warrant. Shakespeare has not proffered his assistance, and really in that case we have no business to help ourselves.

Then there is the voyage to England. Why does Hamlet sail for England? Apparently he does not know himself (there is a vague suggestion of compulsion— again a relic of the older play: he is "without, guarded"; he "must to England"); we do not know; and it seems doubtful if Shakespeare could have given an answer that would have been respectable. He could have given various inadmissible reasons. The actor playing the hero was badly in need of a rest hereabouts; in any case there seemed little else that Hamlet could be made to do just here except go to England; he always had, in the old play or plays, gone to England at this stage of the action and in short there seemed no just cause why he should not keep on going there. Professor Bradley has explained the difficulties attending a Fourth Act in the Shakespearean plan of drama. It comes after the climax and before the play has gathered its last momentum. There is almost compulsorily a lull, an interval not always easy to maintain at an interesting pitch. It is the "delaying" act. Shakespeare surmounts the difficulties here with his customary dexterity. But the hero did present something of a problem. His absence from the action, already prescribed, was perhaps a dramatic convenience as well. He had already delayed; he must still delay; but perhaps better that he should seem vaguely occupied abroad than that he should embarrassingly loiter at home.

Such passages emphasise interestingly the distinction in our drama between dramatic and extra-dramatic causes. We can easily see the purposes which Hamlet's madness serves in the economy of the play. He realises himself in and through it. And what a shield for his satiric comment! From its shelter, with the security of a jester, he launches his barbs. But the motivation of it is another question. So with the English voyage. The reasons for it may be surmised; we are still left to doubt whether these reasons are presentable dramatic reasons.

There are, again, in the play, certain confusions in characterisation, if one scrutinises such matters minutely. We can never, of course, be certain how these arose. But it looks as if they might have arisen from a slightly different cause. Shakespeare was adapting given material. But it is possible, also, that his adaptation was

69

accomplished by stages. If this were so, secondary re-visions may have added minor discords to a plot already a little at odds with itself. Mr G. F. Bradby, for example, has called attention recently to inconsistencies in the account of Horatio. Certainly one has to peer into the character to discover them, but they are, no doubt, there. Putting one group of passages together one gains the impression that Horatio knows all about Elsi-nore, has been brought up with Hamlet and is thoroughly familiar with the Court. But if one selects another group of passages one finds that he was not so familiar with the Court after all and does not know people whom he ought to know. As Mr Bradby says, he appears never to have heard of Yorick or Osric, and Laertes he fails to recognise by sight. He does not even know that the Danes are great drinkers and innocently asks Hamlet if the carousal is a custom. I feel that Mr Bradby drives his discoveries rather hard. One guesses that poor Horatio is deprived momentarily of his knowledge of Danish customs in order that Hamlet may inform him, with philosophical elaboration, about them. But there is no denying that his portraiture (what there is of it apart from Hamlet's eulogium) shifts slightly and wavers. It is as if Shakespeare became absent-minded about Horatio. All this makes it dangerous to attempt (as Professor Allardyce Nicoll has recently done[1]) to draw important conclusions from what one imagines Horatio said and did. Professor Nicoll justifies his procedure by a principle. It is that "the unrevealed or the unknown

[1] *Studies in Shakespeare.*

70

in Shakespeare [has] as great an importance as the known and the revealed". Surely no stronger proof of the unsoundness of such a principle could be adduced than Professor Nicoll's conclusion that one of the causes of Hamlet's indecision is his "reliance on the eminently sane, faithful, and sincere Horatio". Professor Nicoll's view is like this. We see nothing of Horatio between the end of Act I and the play-scene. Just before this begins Hamlet draws his friend aside, pours out that remarkable eulogy, and then tells him what he immediately wants of him (III, ii, 84):

> Even with the very comment of thy soul
> Observe my uncle: if his occulted guilt
> Do not itself unkennel in one speech,
> It is a damned ghost that we have seen.

Afterwards, he says, they will compare notes. Horatio falls in readily with the plan:

> Well, my lord:
> If he steal aught the whilst this play is playing,
> And 'scape detecting, I will pay the theft.

Professor Nicoll finds it notable that Horatio seems to see nothing peculiar in Hamlet's speech, that his answer is so straightforward. The deductions are, first, that he has been informed of what has passed between Hamlet and the Ghost, second, that he has proved somewhat unsympathetic to Hamlet's plans of revenge. Hamlet's words "are in the nature of an appeal". Now we know that Hamlet told Horatio about the murder: he says so (III, ii, 81):

> One scene of it comes near the circumstance
> Which I have told thee of my father's death.

But why Hamlet's words should be considered as in the nature of an appeal, or why we should go out of our way to imagine that Horatio has proved unsympathetic, it is difficult to see. Surely this is again to forget that a play is a play, not raw material for historians. Moreover, those monosyllables which come from Horatio in later portions of the play can be taken far too seriously. Mr Bradby seems nearer the mark when he describes Horatio's chief function as that of a listener who says "ditto" to Hamlet. We can assume that Horatio was thoughtful for and watchful over his friend. But to go, with Professor Nicoll, right behind the scenes, to reconstruct interviews and imagine attitudes, seems a very perilous undertaking. When Hamlet comes to his "is't not perfect conscience" speech (v, ii, 63), Professor Nicoll, continuing to trace this subterranean history of the relations between the friends, takes it to imply "Do you not agree with me *now*?" and finds in Horatio's final words a suggestion that he realises that "his own too great reasonableness has been responsible for much of the disaster"; that is, that he has helped to restrain Hamlet by casting too many doubts on the Ghost. Now we know that Horatio, at the outset of the action, was cautious about accepting the Ghost as genuine. I would suggest that we know, and *can* know, almost nothing else concerning his attitude or his advice. The matter is interesting, once more, for the principle. One agrees with Professor Nicoll that in a drama absences, as well as presences, have value. One knows that characters, after an interval, return changed. One realises the significance of silences on the stage. But it is surely going far to affirm that what does not happen (or is not told) in a drama is as important as what happens (or is told) in it; that the elements which the dramatist has deliberately chosen not to reveal are as significant as those which he has selected as the very stuff of his action. One wonders whether Professor Nicoll, who gives full weight, in theory, to the point of view of audiences, ever stopped to think how an audience was to extricate from the play, while it was in motion, the inner and secret history of the Hamlet-Horatio friendship; just *how* it was to reach its conclusion, in the end, that Horatio's restraining advice (advice, of course, not a word of which has been heard) was in part responsible for the tragedy.

So much, then, for certain difficulties that seem left in our play by the very manner of its origin. The examples could be increased, though it is obvious that any such investigation must be fumbling and conjectural. The very text seems in places to be of an earlier period. It is as if, here and there, an older layer of the play peeps through. But under what microscopes shall we ever elucidate the geology of *Hamlet*?

I should like, however, to conclude this chapter with a note on one other line of enquiry that has yielded interesting suggestions. It enforces the necessity for an historical perspective in viewing the play. Thus, Professor Stoll has shown how much we can learn by judicious comparison of *Hamlet* with other plays of its type; how important, too, for any balanced estimate is

73

an understanding of the distinctively Elizabethan presuppositions that apply. But his general view of the hero
is hardly so convincing as his treatment of some points
of detail. Comparison of literary types is good. But
how if, when all is said, they are not comparable? I
think it would not be very unfair to Professor Stoll[1] to
put his argument (or one of his arguments) like this:
Hamlet is a revenge play; so also is *The Spanish Tragedy*;
then *Hamlet* is in most essential respects like *The Spanish
Tragedy* and its hero is a hero of the same type. But, for
such an equivalence, how much must be ignored! How
much Professor Stoll ignores may be judged from the
fact that Hamlet's first soliloquy is not mentioned by
him; nor is any weight whatever given to the strain of
feeling which that soliloquy announces. The burden of
Professor Stoll's theme is that Hamlet is a "romantic"
hero. Well, but how much more. Deny him "patho-
logy", it still remains true that there is some complexity
in him, some depth (one surely gathers), something remarkable. Professor Stoll is satisfied to find him "fine
and noble", "straightforward and magnanimous", an
"ideal" character, an "intrepid young prince". Nay,
he would even call him "healthy and sturdy". Somehow, we cannot resist the feeling that these are *not* the
words. *Hamlet* is a revenge play; the hero an avenger.
It is something rather different to say that *Hamlet* is
just a revenge play, the hero *only* an avenger. That is,
roughly, I think, what Professor Stoll says.

Professor Stoll would reduce the hero to one type;

[1] *Hamlet: an Historical and Comparative Study.*

74

Professor Schücking[1] would reduce him to another. Professor Stoll finds nothing the matter with Hamlet; Hamlet in Act IV is "himself again", that is to say, is "really what he has always been". Professor Schücking finds a good deal the matter with Hamlet; only it is exactly what is the matter with many other characters in Elizabethan literature. He is a "melancholy" character. Now, again, no one can help being grateful to Professor Schücking for this suggestion. It is important that we should realise that there is an element of convention in Hamlet's character, that even here Shakespeare was, in a sense, drawing on given material, that he was doing over again what had been done before. Our one objection is the same. Professor Schücking, like Professor Stoll, assumes that he could not do it over again differently. After all, we cannot deny our intuitions altogether; and they assure us that, just as Hamlet is not the ideal romantic avenger, so he is not the melancholy man. He has something of both in him, no doubt. But he is neither; he is himself.

[1] *Character Problems in Shakespeare's Plays.*

CHAPTER VII

THE NATURE OF "DELAY"

Professor C. M. Lewis, writing in 1907, made a re-
volutionary suggestion about the problem of *Hamlet*. He
suggested that the problem, in the form in which, since
Goethe and Coleridge, it had always been understood,
might not exist. That is to say, it might be that there is
no psychological cause for the delay. Suppose (and it is
interesting to note how, in such a suggestion, we return
to the neighbourhood of our starting-point, in the comments of Hanmer: the critical wheel comes full circle),
suppose that it amounted to this: that Shakespeare had
a "delay" on his hands that in his freshly conceived plot
was rather awkward to account for; suppose that he
took the easiest way out of the difficulty and, instead of
supplying new motivation, induced us by clever subter-
fuge, disguises and makeshifts to overlook the absence
of motivation; suppose, in short, that instead of re-
explaining the delay he simply left it in his play and
ingeniously, with the magic resources of his art, slurred
it over. It is a supposition that, after our Coleridgean
training, makes us shiver. More recently Professor
Stoll, in his dauntless style, has advocated a similar view.

Now we hesitate to think such things because they
involve a certain condemnation of Shakespeare. When
Professor Stoll has finished with *Hamlet* there is, indeed,
little left of it but a bedraggled and awe-inspiring mass

of wreckage. Professor Lewis is milder. His *Hamlet* still remains a noble object, but it is not quite so noble as we thought it was. It is still, in his figure, a cathedral, but it is a cathedral that begins Saxon, becomes Norman, and ends as Gothic. His view would imply as well that the masonry is not as solid as it appears: some of the pillars are filled with rubble, there is a vein of deception in the workmanship. Our impulse is to reply that it cannot be so. And yet—when Professor Nicoll, voicing again of late the reluctance we all share, speaks in these flat terms: "[Shakespeare], being a great dramatist, obviously must have striven to make such a delay, necessary as it may have been, psychologically possible": we cannot resist a lurking doubt whether the matter is to be so easily disposed of. *Obviously, must,* are strong words; *great dramatist* is a little indefinite. Even if the worst came to the worst and we were compelled to believe that Shakespeare had resorted to such stratagems as Professor Lewis suspects him of and Professor Stoll joyfully lauds him for, perhaps yet we could save greatness for the creator of *Hamlet.* The play would not be precisely the fashion of masterpiece that it is often thought to be. Though the heavens fall we will still claim it masterpiece.

But the question is hardly so serious as that. It would need discrepancies of larger magnitude than these (large as they are) to upset the greatness of *Hamlet.* In the meantime, such suggestions are at least deserving of inspection. I should like, however, to discuss the matter from a slightly different point of view.

77

Now it is interesting, in the first place, to examine a little more closely this conception of "delay". We have noticed more than once the tendency, almost ingrained in *Hamlet* criticism, to treat the play as if it were not a work of art so much as an historical document, as if it were some kind of literal transcript from reality that we could probe into and go behind, as we would probe into and go behind a mass of law-court evidence. We have seen how such a method of investigation leads, in this instance and that, to critical mare's-nests. But I do not think it has been observed (except, in passing, by Professor Stoll) that the delay itself has suffered from a like confusing and distorting scrutiny.

This is a matter of great importance. Delay in real life is one thing; in a drama, another. It is, I suppose, indisputable that one is more impressed by the delay in *Hamlet* when one reads the play than when one sees it; and more still than when one reads it, when one reflects upon it afterwards. A remark of Hudson's is noteworthy. He says that "he has learned by experience that one seems to understand *Hamlet* better after a little study than after a great deal". He draws the inference, how absurd to imagine that we can comprehend this play in a hurry! The inference, of course, is very sound. But the opposite deduction also has its truth, namely, that the only way to grasp the entire *Hamlet* is to understand it quickly, in an embracing impression. Our great handicap (as well as advantage) is that we write with wisdom after the event. One could even suspect that many of the chief difficulties of this play are of the kind that occur to one in afterthought. It is assuredly so with this one. Says Professor Nicoll: "Obviously the first thing which strikes us is the fact that the hero delays so long in achieving his revenge". *When* does it strike us? It strikes us when, in calmness, and after the hurrying scenes have run their course, we begin to reconstruct it all in our minds as it might have been in real life. It is then that we begin to remember things. It is then that the impression of the delay grows on us so powerfully.

It must be emphasised that delay in real life is one thing, in a drama quite another. We know quite well that Hamlet delays two months or so before he kills the King. How do we find this out? We find it out by putting two and two together. We hear from one character in the drama that the old King has been dead not quite two months. Then another character, later, in an unguarded moment, lets slip the information that the King has now been dead "twice two months". We pounce on this. We subtract. Then we follow Laertes. We find that he has been in Paris some time and is now wanting supplies. We collect the evidence bit by bit, we calculate, we reach our conclusions. They are conclusions that, if *Hamlet* were a piece of real life actually occurring, could not be questioned. As it is, they cannot be questioned. Only, they may or may not be of use to us. Laertes could wander all over Europe and yet Hamlet, as far as our impressions go, could in that time have been living a mere two days. In some dramas such things perhaps do not happen; in Shakespearean dramas it is a mere fact that they do. We are here in an Einstein world, where time has strange oddities, where intervals are a delusion and durations a snare. What does it matter that a month or two have gone by between Acts I and II? They have gone by, but not noticeably where Hamlet is; somewhere in another plane of the drama they have gone by.[1] Hamlet at the end of Act I has announced that he will presently put on an antic disposition; in the first scene of Act II we see the initial consequences: he has frightened Ophelia. What has he been doing with himself all the time? It is like asking for news from the fourth dimension. Of course we know that he did several things. He had time to disarrange his attire, and it was perhaps in this interval that he took Horatio into his confidence. But the point to be made is that the interval (apart from one or two such suggestions made about it) has really no dramatic existence. Delay does not exist in a drama simply be-

---

[1] It is true, of course, that Hamlet's "transformation" has been in progress some time before Ophelia is frightened by his "antic disposition". There has been opportunity for Rosencrantz and Guildenstern to be hastily sent for. Ophelia has repelled the Prince's letters and denied him access. Polonius asks her if she has given Hamlet any hard words "of late". I feel, however, that such indications are mere "embedded" delay compared with the powerful impression made by Ophelia's report. Professor Bradley complains that people think that "Hamlet's visit to Ophelia was the first announcement of his madness". It *is* the first announcement of it in the play and arrives as the immediate sequel to Hamlet's revelations, a few moments before, of his intentions. It is hardly to be wondered at that "many readers and, critics imagine that Hamlet went straight to Ophelia's room after his interview with the ghost". The point is that if Shakespeare had in mind strong "delay" values just here, he was no dramatist, for he has not conveyed them.

cause it is (as it were) embedded in it. The delay that exists in a drama is the delay that is displayed. Delay, in any case, does not here quite coincide with time duration, is not the same thing as a mere colourless lapse of days. It is not enough to say that Hamlet procrastinates because, as a matter of fact, and regarding the play somewhat as an historical document, we find that he did not act for two months or so. If he procrastinates, it is because he is shown procrastinating. To put it another way, it is not sufficient that delay should be negatively implicit in the play; it is necessary, for its dramatic existence, that it should be positively demonstrated. The delay, in a word, exists just inasmuch as and just to the degree in which it is conveyed.

It seems to me that if this principle is held in mind, the problem of *Hamlet* looms rather less large. There is, to begin with, less delay to account for. I do not mean merely that we can cease tormenting ourselves with the puzzle of Hamlet's occupations during those mysterious months. Certain scenes and passages which have often been dragged into the problem and made part and parcel of it are seen to have no real relevance to it. It does not, for example, concern us in the slightest that Hamlet, when he ought to be killing his uncle, calmly lectures the players on the intricacies of their art. "How characteristic", says Bradley, "that he appears quite as anxious that his speech should not be ranted as that Horatio should observe its effect on the King." As if Shakespeare were beyond stopping a plot for a moment or two to interpolate (dramatically) some other piece of material that interested him! All this while, of course, Hamlet is delaying. He is delaying while he converses with Ophelia, he is delaying while he welcomes Rosencrantz and Guildenstern, he is delaying while he interviews his mother in her closet. But, of course, in our impressions, he is doing nothing of the kind. How, in the absorption of so much present interest, could we be conscious as well of an inaction beneath the action; how, in the fascination of so much happening could we spare a thought for what is not?

Unless our thought is jogged. It is, in that scene with the mother, where suddenly, in the midst of Hamlet's passionate outburst, the Ghost appears (III, iv, 106):

> HAMLET. Do you not come your tardy son to chide,
> That, lapsed in time and passion, lets go by
> The important acting of your dread command?
> O, say!
> GHOST. Do not forget: this visitation
> Is but to whet thy almost blunted purpose.

Such a passage constitutes a violent reminder. And then there are the famous soliloquies.

The grand problem of *Hamlet* is this: to know exactly how much "delay" there is in the play. I do not mean, to know precisely how long Hamlet delayed, but to know precisely how important in the design of the play the "delay" motive was meant to be. The question, "Why did Hamlet delay?" assumes the other question as solved; but it has never been solved, perhaps is insoluble. One thing, however, seems to be growing clearer: that

82

the motive is not the only motive in the play; that perhaps it is not the central (for we have seen that another competes formidably); that perhaps it is not even a major motive. To go so far may well seem extreme; but it is interesting, once again, to look at the facts.

We have noticed the difficulties in the scene that follows the disclosure of the Ghost. No criticism is sound that ignores the suggestions of imperfect adaptation in this scene. I feel that to approach such a scene in the calm confidence that Shakespeare, seeing that it is such an important scene, *must* therefore have expended his most careful work upon it, *must*, if we had only eyes to see, have made everything clear, is to invite disaster. There are no *musts* about it. Shakespeare ought to have been careful, but if we observe signs that he was not, what can we do but put ourselves on our guard? The antic disposition provides us with something like a false clue at the start; it seems to direct us along the old road of melodrama, although we are presently, in this new play, to swing off at a very wide angle. But if one knew nothing about the play beyond this scene one would imagine that Claudius was a formidable person, difficult to get at, and that the revenge was to be fraught with many dangers against which Hamlet, by these mysterious proceedings, was taking precautions. In short, as we have seen, this incident seems a piece of the old design that was never quite adjusted to the new. It is like a piece of primitive rock projecting through more recent strata. And our only protection is to recognise that this may be so and to beware, accordingly.

At the end of the scene, however, comes the significant couplet:

> The time is out of joint: O cursed spite,
> That ever I was born to set it right!

That it *is* significant, one cannot doubt. But one wishes one could decide precisely in what way. It is a groan at the hatefulness of existence. Life itself has become a burden to Hamlet (and we know, partly, why). Under the burden that weighs him down, duties of revenge, like all other duties, might well lose some of their imperiousness. He is not savouring his revenge (for the savour has gone from all things); he is not anticipating it (as we may imagine his prototype doing) with gusto; we get the impression that he may not, for all his earlier outburst, "sweep" to it. But there is nothing, if we remember the indications we have already had of his state of mind, very puzzling about all this. Nor is it clear why we should be obliged to draw from the words the further inference, namely, that he is already feeling twinges of inadequacy, fearing that he will not, for some reason that he scarcely knows himself, be equal to his task.

Now comes an interval, but we will dispense with conjectures as to how Hamlet spent his time. He put on the antic disposition. The next act goes along. There are no rifts where "delay" might lurk, for all rifts are loaded with dramatic ore. And it is to be remembered that we are really not yet in a position to know what Hamlet is proposing to do about his revenge. "Delay" cannot yet (unless we have second sight) have entered our heads. We come, then, at the very end of the act, to the "O, what a rogue" soliloquy.

What is to be made of this? It would be absurd to attempt to minimize the effect of this passage. There is plenty of "delay" here. And yet it would be, perhaps, just as false to Shakespeare's purpose to underscore heavily all its suggestions. It is so easy to make a "pet" of a passage and then to turn the whole play round until it fits in. How Coleridge did that with Hamlet's few remarks about the "pale cast of thought" and the "thinking too precisely on the event"! However weighty this utterance or that may seem, we are still bound to consider *all* the facts, and while we are contemplating one set to bear in mind the others. It is worth noting, to begin with, that the soliloquy is prompted. We are not compelled to imagine that Hamlet has spent all the interval writhing over some strange torpor that has beset him. The impression is rather different. In any case, as we have seen, it is difficult for us to imagine precisely what Hamlet is doing when we do not see him, and when we do see him he is generally engaged in something that effectively prevents our thinking of his delay. The soliloquy, however, does not clearly imply that Hamlet has been brooding over inadequacy. Rather, this strange behaviour of the player impresses his imagination with a startling contrast. That the actor should have broken down in his speech, shed real tears—"and all for nothing"—while Hamlet himself, with such a living motive, peaks like John-a-dreams and says no word—what a queerness in life! Well, we have had hints of another trouble that is on Hamlet's mind and that might possibly affect his reactions to his new calamity. Are we really made to feel, by the speech, that it is strange that Hamlet has not yet acted? Do we concur in his wonder at himself and join with him in his self-reproaches? A Shakespearean soliloquy is often naïve: and our responses must be naïve; but surely not quite so naïve as that.

It is to be remembered, too, that the soliloquy is not entirely one of self-blame, although no doubt it is our impression of the self-blame that chiefly remains with us. But the impression, though it is by no means neutralised, is a good deal modified by the concluding lines. We have noticed before just how we seem obliged to take these lines which contain the proposal for the play-scene. They do jar, rather, with the lines that have preceded them. It would be pleasant if we could feel that that jar was significant in the sense in which Professor Bradley accepts it. But it is altogether too much of a risk. It seems much more likely, as we have seen, that what we have here is a slight bump in the highway of the plot. Shakespeare has left a little gap between two surfaces. Travelling at speed, we scarcely notice it; when, in our leisurely surveys, we slow down, we feel it.

The soliloquy, then, paves the way (a little roughly) to the play-scene. But we have, intervening, another soliloquy, the "To be". Now this is not, properly speaking, one of the soliloquies of procrastination, although we may allow that it has a relevance for that motive. But its place is rather by the first soliloquy of the play, the "O, that this too too solid flesh would melt". Certainly it is profoundly revealing of Hamlet's mood and, if we have yet begun seriously to wonder why Hamlet delays, furnishes us with a tolerably adequate answer. Hamlet, in his despair, is contemplating a cutting away of the very basis of ethics. For what does this imposed duty, with all other duties, depend on but the assumption that life is worth living: an assumption that Hamlet is now on the verge of denying? The feeling that vengeance (or anything) is worth while presupposes an active belief in life. Hamlet (and we have been given means of knowing why) has almost lost that belief. The point seems to be that so far as the play has gone, there has been, what with one thing and another, not much occasion for surprise in Hamlet's behaviour; nothing, surely, that cannot be received, on our data, without much difficulty; nothing that has really assumed problematical dimensions.

But we have still, of course, the "pale cast of thought" to dispose of. After Hamlet has finished talking about the whips and scorns of time, the fardels, and the dread of the unknown that induces us to continue bearing such trials instead of making our quietus, he draws the moral (III, i, 83):

> Thus conscience does make cowards of us all,
> And thus the native hue of resolution
> Is sicklied o'er with the pale cast of thought,
> And enterprises of great pith and moment
> With this regard their currents turn awry
> And lose the name of action.

What really does he mean? We are still debating this.

Is it just moralising? Or has he, when he says "enterprise", some very particular enterprise in mind—his own, say, of revenge? I would only suggest that there is at least reason for caution. He has not, in the earlier portions of the speech, been thinking of his revenge: at any rate, that has only been part of the "sea of troubles" from which he is considering taking refuge. The sweep of the thought grows wider as he proceeds. The lines in question are like a normal, and somewhat impersonal, generalisation: a philosophical tag to his discourse. They are, in so far, very characteristic of Hamlet, who (like many another Shakespearean character, but in a way all his own) delights to pass from the particular to the general. One thinks of his disquisition to Horatio on the "heavy-headed revel" of the Danes—a speech that does not appear in the Folio, for it is not part and parcel of the plot;—how there he proceeded from his special censure to a wide-reaching conclusion (I, iv, 23):

> So, oft it chances in particular men,
> That for some vicious mole of nature in them,
> As, in their birth...

and so on. It is not denied, of course, that such extra-dramatic utterances (for though they are still dramatic they are extras) often yield much matter. Among them are some of the most pregnant lines in Shakespeare. It has often been observed how much of the essence of the Shakespearean tragedy is held in the nutshell of this very passage (I, iv, 31):

> ...Carrying, I say, the stamp of one defect,
> Being nature's livery, or fortune's star,—

88

> Their virtues else—be they as pure as grace,
> As infinite as man may undergo—
> Shall in the general censure take corruption
> From that particular fault.

And perhaps these other lines of Hamlet's about the resolution sicklied o'er contain some suggestions of what Shakespeare deeply meant to convey about him. But that, again, is something that we must judge from the play as a whole.

The play-scene satisfies Hamlet. He has no more excuse for doubting the authenticity of the Ghost. Now surely he must do something. Well, he does. When he finds the King at prayer he nearly kills him; when he hears him behind the arras he *does* kill him. As it turns out, it is Polonius he has killed, but that is not Hamlet's fault. I know that this seems like burlesquing the sequence, but what can we do? That the deep design which Bradley detects in this series of incidents is really intended I feel we have simply no ground for inferring. Or almost none. All the elements are natural except one. Hamlet's inflamed hate, his savage postponement of the act, the sudden thrust as the "rat" stirs behind the curtain: all this hangs together and bears one meaning on its face and one only. And then the Ghost must needs bring back our doubts.

I do not think any passage in the play is more tantalising than this second exchange between Hamlet and the Ghost. The suggestions are so interesting and yet leave us so perplexed. Hamlet's behaviour in the last quarter of an hour or so has been clear and consistent.

It has been like a recovery. He has roused himself from his broodings to act; he has acted drastically. Yet now he greets the returning Ghost with shamefaced apologies (III, iv, 106):

> Do you not cóme your tardy son to chide,
> That, lapsed in time and passion, lets go by
> The important acting of your dread command?

The Ghost endorses Hamlet's self-censure:

> Do not forget: this visitation
> Is but to whet thy almost blunted purpose.

Now this is the kind of thing that makes *Hamlet*, as a drama, so exasperating. We have been following Shakespeare's lead with good intentions and with every care. We must still believe, in spite of Professor Bradley, that it *was* his lead that we followed. And this is our reward! "Blunted purpose"; "lapsed in time and passion". It is some consolation to find that critics who base their theories on "blunted purposes" are themselves discomposed by this passage. Mr Clutton-Brock will have nothing to do with it. He resorts to "survival" from the old play. In any case, I see no clear way out of the trouble except (the last ludicrous and desperate measure left us) to refuse to take very much notice of the lines. Shakespeare deserves it. It amounts to this: which passage shall we notice? If we take full notice of this one, then we must suspect, in the immediately preceding incidents, dramatic intentions which our impressions do not convey to us. But the conflict of suggestions leaves us very dissatisfied. We know, of course, that the Ghost is speaking from his own point of view. From his point of view, the deed has yet to be done: what Hamlet has planned, what Hamlet has otherwise accomplished, are all irrelevancies. But this does not satisfy us. What tantalises us is our very definite notion that the Ghost is speaking, also, from Shakespeare's point of view, and that when Hamlet says, "lapsed in time and passion", Shakespeare also means lapsed in time and passion. That is our characteristic difficulty with *Hamlet*: to square meanings that will not square; to decide amidst apparently conflicting intentions precisely what it was that Shakespeare did intend. At least it is best to recognise that the difficulty exists.

It recurs, though perhaps in a slightly less insistent form, in our next "delay" passage, which is also our last. We have already seen that to press for reasons—dramatic, psychological reasons—why Hamlet sails for England is to press for what was, as far as we can judge, not supplied. Hamlet sails for England for motives, not of his own, but of Shakespeare's: or perhaps, we may say, of Kyd's. But he does something in Shakespeare that he had probably not done before. He pauses on the way to England to express surprise at himself for going there. We have now to grapple for a moment with the second great "procrastination" soliloquy: the "How all occasions do inform against me" (IV, iv, 32).

It is perhaps worth noting that this soliloquy, like the "O, what a rogue", is prompted. It is not an unstimulated outburst, a welling-up of self-torturings that must find expression and release. No, again a curiosity

of life has struck Hamlet's imagination: the spectacle of
this Prince Fortinbras marching with his army

> To all that fortune, death and danger dare,
> Even for an egg-shell

while he himself, with what "excitements of his reason
and his blood", has done nothing. It is strange. But,
again, is it really strange to us? Fortinbras is, for the
moment, a symbol of exhortation to Hamlet. But do we
really think that Hamlet ought to be like Fortinbras?
Does Hamlet himself, while he uses Fortinbras as a
"spur", not see ironically through and through this
delicate and tender prince who finds quarrels in a straw
and leads twenty thousand men, for a fantasy and trick
of fame, to fight for a plot

> Whereon the numbers cannot try the cause,
> Which is not tomb enough and continent
> To hide the slain?

But, certainly, the "spur" was there; the occasion
informed against Hamlet. Professor Lewis and, after
him, Professor Stoll, elude the obvious suggestions of
this speech very ingeniously. They regard the passage
as, roughly, a kind of stratagem on Shakespeare's part.
After all, Hamlet had been delaying now for some time;
the delay would presently begin to be noticeable. The
English voyage, in particular, might well provoke questions. So Shakespeare, as it were, grasped the nettle
of the difficulty and anticipated our doubts by putting
them in Hamlet's own mouth. He also put promises in
Hamlet's mouth. Hamlet, even if he has done not much

yet (we must remind ourselves that he has done several things) assures us that he will do something soon—

> O, from this time forth,
> My thoughts be bloody or be nothing worth!—

and with this reassurance we sit back contented and agree to overlook his remissness. But Shakespeare was, for once, too clever. He stilled, perhaps, the doubts of his audiences. But the seed sown was to rise up against him: every seed a commentator. And the result of his ingenuity has been the problem of *Hamlet*.

Such a view (Professors Lewis and Stoll differ slightly in their treatment) may well hold some of the truth. We can feel fairly sure that it does not hold all of it. The speech, whatever plot devices it may further, still emphasises a state of mind. But when we ask what elucidation it furnishes of this state of mind, the answer is not so clear (IV, iv, 39):

> Now, whether it be
> Bestial oblivion, or some craven scruple
> Of thinking too precisely on the event,—
> A thought which, quarter'd, hath but one part wisdom
> And ever three parts coward,—I do not know
> Why yet I live to say "this thing's to do,"
> Sith I have cause, and will, and strength, and means,
> To do't.

He has will and strength and means; that is definite. The "bestial oblivion" and "the craven scruple of thinking" are, I think, for all the reams of commentary, doomed to remain indefinite to the end of time. Perhaps that was just what they were meant to be—for we come to this suspicion in the end. Did Shakespeare wish

93

not to pursue that particular motive any farther? After all, we have been shown, apart from "bestial oblivion" and "craven scruple", a good deal of what has been going on in Hamlet's soul. We remember the tremendous pre-occupation that was on him before the Ghost arrived. We know that his thoughts, since the play began, were never single; that there was always that other matter, that other burden. Is "bestial oblivion" the corollary of that other so strong necessity to remember? As for "craven scruple", we do not know what it means. But it seems hardly necessary that we should. Hamlet has delayed because he has had something else (that other thing) to think about. Perhaps the problem requires no further answer than that.

For (and here I return to the primary question) is the problem pressed? There is, concerning this same soliloquy, one other point to be observed. It is not in the First Quarto play. More than that, it is not in the Folio play. That means, apparently, that it was not the custom to speak it in the acting version; it is not now the custom to speak it in the acting version. Now there are, in our play, only two great soliloquies that strongly suggest procrastination, that strongly raise the problem of delay. This is one of them. The other is the soliloquy at the end of Act ii: "O, what a rogue". I will not attempt to decide which of these two soliloquies is the weightier. Professor Bradley, with some suggestion of hesitation, votes for the earlier. If either had to be dispensed with, better, he feels, that it should be the later. But how important the second soliloquy is, especially for a view of the play such as Coleridge's, or Bradley's, may be gauged from the several lines we have been discussing. It is, from all such points of view, a passage of enormous importance. It is one of the twin-pillars of "delay". Now it is easy to say that our concern is merely with the Second Quarto; that the play, as cut down for acting, means nothing to us. It does mean something. The omission of the soliloquy means this: that if Shakespeare intended his play to be, above all, about procrastination, if he meant it above all things for a study in "delay", he was misunderstood almost at the beginning. The actors of his own time misunderstood him; or, if they understood him, decided that it was of no use trying to convey his meaning. I suppose it is obvious that no performance of *Hamlet* ever has succeeded, ever will or can succeed, in conveying that meaning.

This is not to deny procrastination. Of course there is procrastination. But it is not everywhere in the play, the play is not compounded of it, it is not the theme of themes: at least I fail to see how it can be considered so. The "How all occasions" soliloquy is the last clear and obvious suggestion of procrastination that we have. The fifth act is full of varied interest. Hamlet returns. In the second half of the act the current of events becomes a swirl and we are swept to the culmination. And when we look back over the course of the play, it is not on one long delay that we think. The changing spectacle, the absorbing story, have left us space only now and again for a glimpse of these doubts and hesitations. They are there, they are in the design; they are not the design.

95

CHAPTER VIII

CONCLUSION

I would suggest, then, that the question "Why did Hamlet delay?", instead of being *the* question about Hamlet, is a question that in our immediate experience of the play (which is our all-important experience) does not, after all, very seriously arise. No one can deny the positive indications of delay; they are not, however, quite so numerous or quite so urgent as one might be led to think from some of the critical accounts; and their cumulative effect is not, perhaps, so powerful as has been assumed. The play is not dyed in delay. Now that means, simply, that the problem of the inaction recedes. It does not vanish. But it becomes less obtrusive.

Nor does it seem necessary, even if we suppose that the inaction is accounted for, by Shakespeare, rather less certainly, with rather less logic, than it is accounted for by Coleridge and Bradley, that we should rush into a kind of critical atheism, proclaiming the shattering of our belief in the dramatist. Dramas are of many kinds. We have no reason to require of Shakespeare that every play should match a set technique. The inaction (as much of it as is dramatically urgent, as much of it as Shakespeare permits to become stuff of the drama) is accounted for, when all is said, with fair sufficiency. It does not worry us, unless we let it worry us. We take it in our stride. And it was surely open to Shakespeare, when he wished, to keep motives subdued, as it was open to him, when he wished, to enforce them.

We still, of course, have our difficulties: plenty of them. Some of these, as we have seen, seem inherent in the design. The play, from one point of view, is a tremendous *tour de force*. An old plot is wrenched to new significances, significances, in places, that to the end it refuses to take. It was, perhaps, inevitable that the play should show signs, in fissures and strain, of all this forceful bending. There are other difficulties that we can hardly venture to account for. Motives vaguely indicated ("blunted purpose", "lapsed in time") fade, seem somehow thwarted in their working out. We are left to surmises. Chords are sounded, dimly, suggestively, then become blurred. We seem to gain partial visions of intentions not clearly formulated. (How it would have helped us, supposing Shakespeare strongly meant "delay", if he had made Horatio give a hint, in aside of just four words! Indeed, the failure, in such a case, to make use of Horatio for explanatory comment —never needed more than here!—is well-nigh incredible.) But what would *Hamlet* be without its puzzles: the eternal piquancy of its imperfection?

Imperfection. For the play, after all, is just a play: a work of art with a design that is deceptive and intricate and somewhat misleading. We are discouraged if we cannot trace the design as evenly as we could wish, we are disappointed if we find the pattern a little mixed and bewildering. But at least we must keep to the design as it appears, abide by the patterns as we find them.

Nothing is to be gained by compelling system from what is not system. If the filaments are not everywhere tight, it is not for us to tighten them; if the design relaxes, we cannot put it right.

But there is an inveterate temptation to try. We are for ever discovering new causes for Hamlet's inaction. Professor Nicoll the other day discovered one more. He suggests that a chief cause was Hamlet's ambition, or rather, his fear of his ambition: more precisely, his sincerity. The King speaks once of Hamlet's "pride"; Hamlet himself makes a remark to Rosencrantz about "lacking advancement"; he declares, again, to Ophelia that he is "proud, revengeful, ambitious"; and later (v, ii, 65) refers to the King as one who has "Popp'd in between the election and [his] hopes". Hamlet, then, has a strongly ambitious spirit, distrusts it, and fears that if he murders his uncle it may be, deep in his heart, for his own ends. So, he delays. Surely it will not do. Those few wisps of suggestions, artificially put together, make in the total design a thread that is absolutely invisible. Nothing is more obvious than that such an idea was never in Shakespeare's head. No, it seems pretty clear that we can find out no more secrets about Hamlet's motives. A play is not a mine of secret motives. We persist in digging for them; what happens usually is that our spade goes through the other side of the drama.

Is it, finally, of very great moment that we must admit these difficulties? The play, in spite of its discrepancies, has a fine harmony. Can we look usually in Shakespeare for the precise and narrow consistency that distinguishes the work of some other great literary craftsmen? Invincible logic of plot was scarcely his special glory. How different is, say, a novel by Henry James, the technique so deliberate, the fashioning so conscious; the work *sound* through and through! Shakespeare is rarely *sound* in that sense: how majestically careless, in comparison, he can be! He gives us things that were beyond James's range: he does not give us just that. To look for it is rather to wrong him. We know what, among other things, he has given us in *Hamlet*: the portrait of a man who seems to express (and the more in his sufferings and his disasters) all that Shakespeare found of greatest beauty and worth in the human spirit. There is no one, in history or in literature, like Hamlet. All that humanity is, all that humanity might be, seem figured in him. It is no wonder if we find it a task of some difficulty to pluck out all the mysteries of his soul.

INDEX OF WRITERS

Made in United States
Orlando, FL
03 June 2023

33772434R00065